Study Skills for Students with Dyslexia

Education at SAGE

SAGE is a leading international publisher of journals, books, and electronic media for academic, educational, and professional markets.

Our education publishing includes:

- accessible and comprehensive texts for aspiring education professionals and practitioners looking to further their careers through continuing professional development

- inspirational advice and guidance for the classroom

- authoritative state of the art reference from the leading authors in the field

Find out more at: **www.sagepub.co.uk/education**

→ **SAGE Study Skills**

Study Skills for Students with Dyslexia

Edited by
Sandra Hargreaves

2nd Edition

SAGE

Los Angeles | London | New Delhi
Singapore | Washington DC

SAGE Publications Ltd
1 Oliver's Yard
55 City Road
London EC1Y 1SP

SAGE Publications Inc.
2455 Teller Road
Thousand Oaks, California 91320

SAGE Publications India Pvt Ltd
B 1/I 1 Mohan Cooperative Industrial Area
Mathura Road
New Delhi 110 044

SAGE Publications Asia-Pacific Pte Ltd
3 Church Street
#10–04 Samsung Hub
Singapore 049483

Library of Congress Control Number: 2011934287

British Library Cataloguing in Publication data

A catalogue record for this book is available from the British Library

ISBN 978-1-4462-0286-9
ISBN 978-1-4462-0287-6 (pbk)

Typeset by C&M Digitals (P) Ltd, Chennai, India
Printed in India at Replika Press Pvt Ltd
Printed on paper from sustainable resources

Contents

About the CD-ROM

A CD-ROM accompanies the book, and it contains:

- The whole text of the book in Microsoft Word. This has been done to make the book as accessible as possible for students with dyslexia and those with other Specific Learning Difficulties. This allows you to:
  - have the text of the book read out to you using a text reader such as ClaroRead Plus or Text HELP Read & Write
  - change the colour of the background, font style and size.
- Access student planners, essay templates and like materials supplied as Word, Excel files, etc. so that you can copy and edit them.
- Access a number of internet shortcuts for each chapter which offer further information, templates and additional help.

Throughout the book, you will see this CD icon used ⊙. This indicates that there is electronic material available on the accompanying CD-ROM.

About the Editor and the Contributors

The editor

Sandra Hargreaves was the Course Leader for both the MA SpLD and the PGDip in Assessment for SpLD (Dyslexia) at London Metropolitan University, where she was a Teaching Fellow. In addition she was Module Leader for Supporting Adult Learners with SpLD, which is part of the MA SpLD run jointly by the Dyslexia Association in Singapore and London Metropolitan University. She is the Director of Mind Aligned (www.mindaligned.org). Mind Aligned is a service which covers a range of different activities including diagnosing dyslexia and supporting dyslexic adults both in higher education and the workplace. Sandra has been involved in dyslexia support at Thames Valley University, the Inner London Probation Service and Uxbridge College. She previously worked for many years in Australia at Macquarie University in the Teacher Education Programme where she was the Course Leader of the Secondary English Team.

She has Associate Membership of the British Dyslexia Association in Further and Higher Education (AMBDA FE/HE) and a Practising Certificate from the Professional Association of Teachers of Students with SpLD (PATOSS). Sandra has been involved with education throughout her career. After initial training as an English teacher at the University of Newcastle in Australia, she completed both an MA and MEd at the University of Sydney. She has undertaken all her training in dyslexia in the UK. She is also dyslexic.

Her interest in education has been extensive. She has travelled to the United States, where she had a Fulbright Scholarship and the UK where she enjoyed an educational award sponsored by the British Council. She has given papers at international conferences in the USA, UK, Europe, Singapore and Australia.

The contributors

All contributors completed the Postgraduate Certificate: Teaching Adult Dyslexic Learners in Higher and Further Education at London Metropolitan University and are all working as dyslexia tutors in London universities.

Peri Batliwala works as a dyslexia support tutor at Middlesex University and freelances at a number of other London universities and colleges. She started her professional life working for international development charities as an administrator and sub-editor for many years. After having a family she undertook higher degrees and retrained as a secondary English teacher, a basic skills tutor and most recently, a dyslexia support tutor.

Paula Baty (née Dawson) has a private practice, Meta-Learning (www.meta-learning.co.nz), which provides tuition, assessment and consultancy services for students with specific learning difficulties. She also works part-time at the University of Auckland, New Zealand, as a tutor and assessor for students with SpLDs. Prior to that, Paula spent a number of years in London, working as a dyslexia adviser and tutor at various universities, including the London School of Economics and Political Science, Kingston University and London South Bank University. Paula has an MA in Education (Specific Learning Difficulties) from London Metropolitan University, for which she received a University Prize for Academic Excellence – Best Masters Award with Distinction, First Place. She also holds a BA in English from Massey University, and a Trinity Certificate in Teaching English to Speakers of Other Languages (TESOL).

Helen Birkmyre has worked as a freelance dyslexia tutor at Goldsmiths College London and The Dyslexia Teaching Centre in Kensington. She read history at Goldsmiths and completed an MA in Cultural History. She completed her Postgraduate Certificate in Dyslexia Tutoring at London Metropolitan University. She is now working freelance at the Dyslexia Assessment and Consultancy Centre in Kennington; City and Guilds of London Art School; and Central Saint Martins School of Art and Design. She is also studying for a BA in Fine Art (3D) at Central Saint Martins.

John Brennan is a dyslexia support tutor at University of the South Bank and Kingston University. After education at Downside and Brasenose College, Oxford, John worked in IT until 1999 in London with significant periods in Belgium and Holland. Two of the more interesting projects John worked on were the traffic management systems for the Channel Tunnel terminals and Wester Schelde estuary.

Judith Cattermole works part-time as a dyslexia support tutor for students at Middlesex and City Universities in London. She has a particular interest in helping dyslexic students who are experiencing problems with their numeracy skills. In addition Judith works as a senior manager in Learning Resources at Middlesex University and is a qualified librarian with over 30 years of experience.

Jamie Crabb is the Disability Services Coordinator at Central School of Speech and Drama (Central), University of London. He also works as a freelance specialist 1:1 dyslexia support tutor, and as an assistive technology tutor. After completing his BA (Hons) Drama and Education at Central in 2002 he worked as Project Coordinator for the Metropolitan Police Service Safer Schools Project in Haringey, and as a visiting lecturer on the BA (Hons) Drama, Applied Theatre and Education at Central.

Jane Davis has worked for colleges and as a private tutor for 15 years, covering ESOL, Basic Skills, Learning Support and English Literature and Language. She has also published poetry and had plays performed. She is currently working for Roehampton University, Regent's College and a number of private agencies as a freelance SpLD support tutor. She has a strong interest in the emotional as well as cognitive aspects of study and in how individual differences affect the motivation to learn.

Kay McEachran works as a dyslexia support tutor at Goldsmiths' and Queen Mary, University of London. She completed a BA (Hons) in History at Goldsmiths before going on to do an MA in Politics and Government at London Guildhall University. In 2005 she completed her PGC: TADLHE at London Metropolitan University and is currently studying for the Postgraduate Diploma for the Assessment of Specific Learning Difficulties (Dyslexia), also at London Metropolitan University.

Cheri Shone came to do a degree as a mature student as a direct result of her dyslexia. She completed a BSc Hons Psychology and went on to do a Postgraduate Diploma in Counselling Skills and a PGC in Teaching Adult Dyslexia Learners in Higher Education. She is currently tutoring at the Working Men's College and London South Bank University. She has a keen interest in the use of technology to support the weaknesses of the dyslexic student and how to integrate technology into tutorial support sessions.

Acknowledgements

Every effort has been made to seek permission where material has been known to come from specific sources. The following permissions are gratefully acknowledged:

Diagram of Cognitive Styles and Learning Strategies (p. 15) reproduced by kind permission from *Cognitive Styles and Learning Strategies* by Richard Riding and Stephen Rayner, David Fulton Publishers, 1998, p. 98.

References to Mind Maps™ (pp. 17, 30, 33, 35, 52, 57, 58, 64, 85, 135, 136, 139, 145, 150) reproduced by kind permission from *The Mind Map Book* (rev. edition) by Tony Buzan with Barry Buzan, BBC Active, 2006.

Visual Memory Pegs (p. 19) reproduced by kind permission from *Make the Most of Your Mind* (rev. edition) by Tony Buzan, Pan Books, 1988.

Auditory Memory Pegs (p. 20) reproduced by kind permission from *Use Your Head* (4th edition) by Tony Buzan, BBC, 1995.

The Cornell Note-making System (pp. 31–32) reproduced by kind permission from *How to Study in College* (7th edition) by Walter Pauk, Houghton Mifflin, 2001, p. 201.

Q Notes Template (CD-ROM, Chapter 3) reproduced by kind permission from *Tools for Thought* by Jim Burke, Heinemann, 2002.

The Point Evidence Comment method of paragraph writing (Chapter 6) reproduced by kind permission from *The Good History Student's Handbook*, edited by Gilbert Pleuger, Sempringham, 2000.

Abstract Writing (p. 73, CD-ROM Chapter 6) reproduced by kind permission from the Online Writing Lab of Purdue University.

There are many people whom I would like to thank who have been indispensable to the development and production of this book. First my grateful thanks are due to all the contributors, who gave their time to develop chapters on topics in which they had expertise. My special thanks go to John Brennan who was responsible for the systematic layout of the chapters at the draft stages and his patient advice regarding all aspects of ICT culminating in his compilation of the CD-ROM. Secondly I am greatly indebted to all the students who have used the strategies in this book and who have been willing to write and speak about their experiences in the case studies. I would also like to thank both Jude Bowen and Thea Watson for their honest but supportive comments and advice during the editorial and production process. Finally I would like to thank all my family and friends who have unstintingly supported my efforts on this book and for their unswerving belief that I would complete it.

This book is dedicated to dyslexic students and those with other Specific Learning Difficulties who have struggled with the demands of student life. I hope that the strategies we have suggested will bring success.

How to Use this Book

This book is for students with dyslexia and has been designed to be used independently. It provides strategies to help dyslexic students and those with other Specific Learning Difficulties such as dyspraxia but would also be helpful for a wide range of students, for what is specifically useful for dyslexic students is useful for everyone. If you would like more information about learning difficulties, you should approach the Disability and Dyslexia Service at your college. As well as giving help and material resources, these services will assist you to apply for the Disabled Students' Allowance (DSA) if you are eligible for it. For information, go to: www.direct.gov.uk/en/DisabledPeople/EducationAndTraining/HigherEducation/DG_10034898

It is always a good idea to be proactive about your learning difficulties and to inform your lecturers and tutors so that they can adjust their teaching practices by providing notes (preferably in digital format) and prioritised reading lists in advance and allowing the use of recorders. Remember that you are not asking for favours, but for your rights under the Disability Act. Your lecturers and tutors have an obligation to make 'reasonable adjustments' to accommodate your individual needs. See, for example: http://www.nottingham.ac.uk/academicsupport

A CD-ROM accompanies the book which contains:

- The whole text of the book in Microsoft Word. This has been done to make the book as accessible as possible for students with dyslexia and those with other Specific Learning Difficulties. This allows you to:
  - have the text of the book read out to you using a text reader such as ClaroRead Plus or TextHELP Read & Write
  - change the colour of the background, font style and size.

- Student planners, essay templates and like materials supplied as Word, Excel files, etc. so that you can copy and edit them.
- A number of internet shortcuts for each chapter which offer further information, templates and additional help.

The colour background of the book itself has been designed for dyslexic students, who often find that it is hard to read black text on a white background.

You can change the background colour of the text in this book, if it doesn't suit you, by using a coloured overlay. Try different colours to see which suits you by trialling different coloured plastic folders.

The text has been **emboldened** in sections, which appears as a contrasting colour on the CD. The purpose is twofold, to:

- enable you to **scan** (see Chapter 4, 'Reading Strategies and Speed Reading') the book for the **main ideas**
- encourage you to use **highlighting** as a note-making **technique** (see Chapter 3, 'Note Taking and Note Making').

Colour has been used throughout the text and in a number of figures – these are available on the accompanying CD-ROM.

This book is a collection of **strategies** and **techniques** (such as **highlighting**) which have been collected over many years and from many sources. I hope that they will help you and that having compiled them into a study guide you will have the strategies at your disposal to cope with the academic demands of your course. The book is an edited collection of chapters containing strategies from a range of tutors. All the **strategies have been trialled and found to be successful.** All the contributors have completed the Postgraduate Certificate: Teaching Adult Dyslexic Learners in Higher and Further Education at London Metropolitan University.

The book has been designed to help students with the demands of college or university life. As such, it allows readers to select according to their immediate needs. So you can go to Chapter 5, 'Answering Essay Questions' if you need help with a forthcoming essay, or to Chapter 6, 'Structuring Different Writing Genres' for a report. You may find, however, that by systematically reading the whole book your organisation and study strategies will generally improve, and you will not feel under so much pressure as you approach deadlines.

This material has been used over many years, and it is not always possible to know where it originated and who should be acknowledged for the original idea. In some cases I have observed the strategies being used with dyslexic students by excellent tutors working in the field and I would like to acknowledge all the useful work that goes on in dyslexia tutorials all over the country.

The aim of the book is, as Alan Bennett says so effectively through the voice of the English teacher at the end of *The History Boys*: 'Pass it on … Pass it on'. That surely is the aim of all good education so that those who have learnt the skills can share them with those who have not as yet encountered them.

A final point to remember – don't let yourself become overwhelmed by the demands of your education. Don't give up but try another strategy, another way to learn something new. I am dyslexic. I only found out I was dyslexic when I moved to the UK and started to work in this field. The more I worked with dyslexic adults, the more I realised that I had experienced the same problems since childhood, many of which I have managed to overcome using some of the strategies now incorporated in this book.

Sandra Hargreaves, AMBDA, FRSA
BA, Dip Ed, MA, MEd, ADS Cert

1

Managing Your Workload

Jamie Crabb, Jane Davis and Sandra Hargreaves

developmental objectives

This chapter:

- explains the importance of developing organisational skills
- explores self-esteem, managing well-being and motivation
- outlines the overall structure of college life including the main things you have to consider
- suggests ways of planning your workload so that you can complete assignments on time and still enjoy some leisure and exercise
- introduces useful new technology and software to help with organisation
- provides examples and templates of weekly and semester timetables (CD-ROM)
- provides templates of helpful forms such as 'To do' lists (CD-ROM).

College lifestyle

If you have never been to college or university before, you will find it a very great change from the more organised environment of secondary school. Apart from your timetabled lectures, tutorials, seminars and examinations, **how you organise yourself will be up to you**. If you don't organise yourself early in your student life, you can find that you get very behind in all your commitments and this can lead to stress as well as the possibility of failing modules, resubmissions and resits. **Remember, an organised student is a successful student**. You may need to extend or develop effective systems of organisation to support you through your course and it would be useful to explore these with a tutor. There are suggestions offered later in this chapter.

During your study, you will find learning and committing to memory is made easier if you use **multi-sensory methods**. This simply means using strategies that draw on as many of the senses as possible in your learning. Remember that colour, image, sound, movement, the use of the voice, etc. can all play a useful part in making learning personal and enjoyable (see Chapter 2 'Understanding Your Preferred Learning Style'). In addition, new technologies and software can be enabling tools for your study (see 'Using new technologies and software', below). 'My Study Bar', developed by Regional Support Centre, Scotland and North East, combines excellent free software tools, which are an excellent starting point for exploring how technology can support your study: http://eduapps.org/?page_id=7

Self-esteem and well-being

The new challenges presented by college life may sometimes have an emotional impact. It is possible that you may experience personal issues, or difficulties engaging with methods of teaching and understanding assessment tasks when they do not match your preferred learning style (see Chapter 2). Difficulties during study can lead to stress, feelings of anxiety and low self-esteem, which can further affect your ability to manage your study.

As a result, it is important to understand that it is **your responsibility to monitor and manage your personal well-being** throughout your course. Well-being relates to **your ability to manage difficulties and stressful feelings** in order to realise your goals.

Learning to be mindful of your well-being can be an important skill to develop during your study. Explore sitting or active meditation practices, yoga, dance and individual sports such as swimming which encourage **a positive mental and physical attitude**. Try not to ignore difficulties – learn to be aware of them and seek support. This can be an important step in developing new strategies to become a more successful learner.

Remember – being mindful of your well-being should be **proactive!** Important things to be mindful of to ensure your well-being should include:

- taking regular exercise
- keeping a regular sleep pattern
- taking advantage of student clubs, study and support groups
- budgeting to avoid financial difficulties
- eating regular healthy meals to ensure good nutrition

2

- factoring in time for weekly leisure and social activities
- moderating your alcohol consumption.

Your student union and student support services can be a useful resource to advise you how to manage difficulties and maximise your well-being. It is important to remember that if you experience difficulties:

- related to study – consider exploring these with an academic tutor or a dyslexia support tutor
- of a personal nature – consider approaching your student support services who will be able to advise you of the support available (e.g. counselling or money advice).

Remember – being responsible for managing your well-being is important for successful study.

(GO to CD-ROM Well-being and Mindfulness Information)

Motivation

Motivated students who have a positive, proactive attitude towards their studies manage stress and challenges better and are more likely to achieve. Genuine interest in your subject is crucial, but even the most enthusiastic student can sometimes be demotivated by workload pressure or an unexpectedly poor grade. If you are focusing too much on your difficulties, **challenge negative thoughts** by writing down a more realistic view of the situation: **use critical feedback as an opportunity for development**. For example replace

I can't write introductions
with
I can look at models, get advice from my tutor and learn how to improve my introductions

(GO to CD-ROM Managing Challenges Example and Template)

Effective ways of boosting motivation include:

- focusing on the benefits of your course

(GO to Course Benefits Template on CD-ROM)

- challenging negative thoughts
- goal setting and rewarding yourself
- breaking down assignment tasks so they are more manageable
- exploring creative and multi-sensory study methods that suit your learning style (see Chapter 2)
- developing good relationships with academic and support tutors

- finding a study partner for mutual support with motivation
- avoiding burn-out by taking time to relax, socialise and exercise.

Goal setting and breaking down tasks

It is motivating to identify your **long-term** and **short-term goals**.

○ **(GO to SMART (Specific, Measurable, Achievable, Realistic, Time-bound) Goals Example and Template on CD-ROM)**

For example, make a poster list of one of your long-term goals – e.g.what you hope to achieve at the end of your course or term. A long-term goal might be:

'become a practising clinical psychologist'

The next step is to break your long-term goal into realistic, more manageable short-term goals. Short-term goals are steps towards your long-term objective, e.g.:

'develop essay writing skills'

These smaller goals can be broken down further into sub-steps to identify achievable tasks. You can do this independently or with a tutor. Breaking down goals and assignment tasks puts you in control.

○ **(Go to Task Breakdown Example and Template on CD-ROM)**

Remember to reward yourself when you achieve a goal. This can be a simple treat like having your favourite food, watching your favourite DVD or a fun night out with a friend or partner. Aim to be mindful and **notice** how much you are learning and give yourself credit for the progress you make. Be flexible: it is demotivating if you start to criticise yourself for not reaching particular targets.

Main features of college study

- Weekly lectures, tutorials, seminars, practical sessions or workshops on campus.
- Assignments or essays, reports, journals, presentations. This may include individual and group work.
- Examinations.
- Independent study in the library or at home.

The timetabled elements of your course may vary according to whether, for example, you are following a science subject, with a lot of practical work or arts and humanities, where there will be more free time intended for reading and writing independently.

Tips

- Visit student services for information about accommodation, finance and support.
- Get to know your college environment well, so you can locate classes easily and factor in sufficient travel time if you live off campus.
- Attend a library induction and get to know your subject librarian and other support staff.
- Ensure you attend any IT training or inductions and study skills sessions.
- Register with a local doctor.

Methods of organising your workload

With a little organisation, you can control the pace of your work without feeling overwhelmed. Useful strategies for managing both coursework, revision and study folders include:

- A **colour-coded list of assignments** with word limits and deadlines and assessment value – e.g. 30% of module marks.
- Week to view diaries or **printable weekly timetables**, including scheduled classes, independent study, break and leisure activities. Use a different colour for each course module.
- A **semester or term planner** for your wall. The timetable and term planners will show you how much time you have available for study. Assignment deadlines and examination dates should be entered so you are clear about how much time you have to meet your deadlines.
- A **weekly to do list**.
- Use different coloured folders for storing notes for each of your modules: use dividers and label folders clearly so you can find notes easily.
- Manage computer files by organising them in folders for each year and subfolders for terms and their modules. Create further subfolders for pieces of work, research and assignments. Remember to use meaningful titles for your folders and files and ensure you back up your work regularly.
- Manage your emails by organising them into folders and subfolders.

The CD-ROM that accompanies this book contains Microsoft Word and Excel examples, templates and guidance for these organisational strategies. See also 'Using new technologies and software', below.

Meeting your deadlines

When you have created your timetables, planners and an assignment list, you can start to look at the assignments in more depth, and break them down into smaller, more manageable task units.

(GO to SMART Goals Example and Template on CD-ROM)

The most obvious stages are:

1 Unpacking the essay question/understanding assignment criteria.
2 Brainstorming or concept mapping to clarify your ideas.
3 Reading, researching or performing an experiment.
4 Making notes and/or managing quantitative and qualitative data.
5 Organising your material into sequential paragraphs (essay) or into report headings (scientific writing).
6 Writing the essay or report.
7 Proofreading and re-drafting.
8 In general it is helpful to allow four to six weeks for complex assignments (3,000 to 5,000 words) and for coursework that requires a lot of research/data analysis.

Tips

- Become more aware of how long it takes you to perform certain tasks. For example, you can create plans quickly but need more time for reading and note-making. Factor this in to your task breakdown.
- Keep an activity log (**Go to CD-ROM Activity Log Example and Template**) to see how effectively you are spending your time – are you focusing your energy on tasks that will get you results or spending too long on unimportant activities?
- Try to spend more time on assignments that weigh heavily in your assessments: e.g. you should spend more time on an assignment that is worth 50% than one worth 10%.
- Practice setting priorities – the website MindTools has some useful information and templates (http://www.mindtools.com/).
- When writing to do lists, brainstorm everything you need to do then number the tasks according to their importance or urgency.

(GO to Urgent/Important Guide and Prioritised To Do List Example and Template on CD-ROM)

Using new technologies and software

New technologies and software can be a breath of fresh air to help you manage and organise your time and information during your study.

Time planning and email management

Computer-based and internet calendars can be useful tools to aid time planning. Microsoft Outlook, which is part of the Microsoft Office suite, is a computer-based organisational program with integrated calendar, email and task management. Mozilla's Sunbird is a free computer based alternative. Google Calendar is an excellent free online calendar, which you can access from any computer or mobile device that has internet access. Such programs can be used to visually plan and prioritise your study time, set up reminders and create 'to do' lists.

Portable devices

Personal Digital Assistants (PDA), Tablet Computers, some Mobile Phones and Smart Phones are excellent portable organisers. These devices integrate a combination of internet and email access, calendar, notebook, address book, alarm clock, voice recorder, audio player, GPS maps and in some cases mobile communication. Examples of these devices include:

- Windows Phone.
- iPod Touch, iPhone and iPad.
- Blackberry Phone.
- Mobile phones and Tablets running Google Android.

These devices can synchronise with your computer and online calendars, task lists, notes and documents, enabling mobile access, editing and helpful reminders wherever you are.

File management and backup

USB (Universal Serial Bus) memory sticks are extremely useful as a means of transferring data from home to university computers. However, **try not to rely on them as a form of backup**. A good investment is an **external hard drive**, which can be set up to backup your computer files regularly.

7

The internet has made it possible to backup files you use regularly online so that you can access and manage them in different venues. **Dropbox** is an excellent example, offering 2GB of free storage space and instant backup and syncronisation of files between your computers and mobile devices. Apple computers and devices offer 5GB of free storage with iCloud. Additionally, **Windows Live Skydrive with Office Live**, and **Google Documents** are internet 'Cloud' based software, which enable backup and editing of files using any computer or mobile device with internet access.

⊙ **(GO to Using Dropbox on CD-ROM)**

Organising research

Free organisational software can be an empowering tool to help you organise your research. **Evernote** is an excellent research tool that enables you to create a **searchable archive** to capture and organise your notes, information from webpages, images and documents using any computer or mobile device. Integrating the **Mozilla Firefox** internet browser with the **Delicious Firefox Bookmarking tool** can help you to capture and organise websites to create a **personalised searchable archive**. **Zotero** is a Firefox add-on that allows you to extract bibliographic information from library catalogues and websites to create a **personalised bibliographic catalogue**. Zotero integrates with Microsoft Word and Open Office to make adding citations and bibliographies simple and systematic.

Exploring new technologies and software can save you a lot of time and effort managing your study. With a little practice, the process of organising your studies can become simpler and more efficient. The CD-ROM that accompanies this book contains web links, templates and further guidance.

⊙ **(GO to Using New Technologies and Software Information and Guides on CD-ROM)**

In Figure1.1 four basic striking colours are used to distinguish the modules: brown, purple, aqua and blue. The list has been compiled in Microsoft Word. Notice the use of:

- a large font the student likes, in this case Comic Sans
- consistent colour coding
- scoring out of completed work; this gives a sense of achievement and draws attention to the next item on the list
- inclusion of assignment word limits and value.

```
November '11      WK 6

Thursday 10ᵗʰ    TS 101:    PProduction Journal      (2,000 words, 20%)


                  WK 8

Friday 25ᵗʰ      AT 211     Practical Report         (3,500 words, 40% )

DECEMBER '11     WK 10

Friday 9ᵗʰ       ND 214     Video Analysis           (2,000 words, 60%)
Friday 9ᵗʰ       ND 214     Presentation on Video Analysis, (40%)


                  WK 11

Tuesday 13ᵗʰ     AT211      Group Presentation       (10 mins total)
                            (Liam, Caroline, Mario, Joanne)

Friday 16ᵗʰ      MS 220:    Personal Research Essay (3,500, 50%)

JANUARY '12      WK 12

Friday 6ᵗʰ       MS 220:Learning Portfolio           (3,000 words, 50%)
```

Figure 1.1   Colour Coded Assignment List – an Example (see CD-ROM)

(GO to Microsoft Word and Excel Planner Examples and Templates on CD-ROM)

Note the use of consistent colour coding for timetabled sessions and independent study for each module e.g.: light green = time spent working on ND214 (Figure 1.2) and pink = time spent working on EiC (Figure 1.3) and in the semester or term planner (Figure 1.4).

(GO to Year Planner on CD-ROM)

To do lists

These are very simple to compile and many highly efficient dyslexic and non-dyslexic people use them all the time. All you have to do to compile your list is put down the day or date for the deadline and tick off the tasks as you complete them. Table 1.1 was created in Microsoft Word and can be added to at any time by simply adding rows.

(GO to To Do List Templates on CD-ROM)

Table 1.1   To Do list

To Do	Day/Time	Completed
Group presentation with Radek and Martin	Thursday 10.00	✓
Reading for Psychology Seminar	Tuesday 3.00pm	
Birthday Present for Mum	asap	

Time	Monday	Tuesday	Wednesday	Thursday	Friday	Saturday	Sunday
9			TS 101 Workshops		MS 220 Seminar		2 hrs
10	ND 214 Lecture	TS 101 Lecture	Break	AT211 Lecture	Break		Break
11			2 hrs		1.5 hrs		1.5 hrs
12						Day Off	
1pm	Lunch	Lunch	Lunch	Lunch	Lunch	Work	Lunch
	Dyslexia	Library	Journey home				
2	Journey home		1.5 hrs	ND214 Seminar	1.5 hrs		1.5 hrs
3	2 hrs	MS 220 Lecture	Break		Break		Break
4			2 hrs	Break	2 hrs		2 hrs
5	Dinner	Journey home		1.5 hrs			
		Dinner					
6	1.5 hrs		Dinner	Dinner	Dinner		Dinner
7		2 hrs	2 hrs	Dance			2 hrs
8				Pilates			
9	Yoga	Break	Break		Night Off		Break
		1 hr	1 hr	Break			1 hr
10							

Figure 1.2   Weekly planner – semester 1

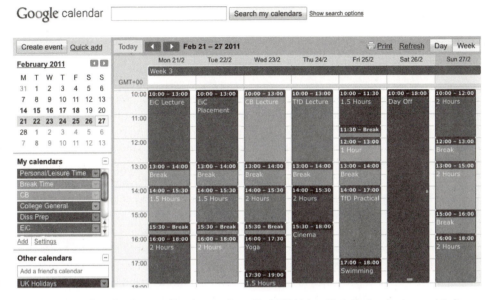

Figure 1.3   Google calendar weekly planner (See CD-ROM Using New Technologies and Software Information and Guides)

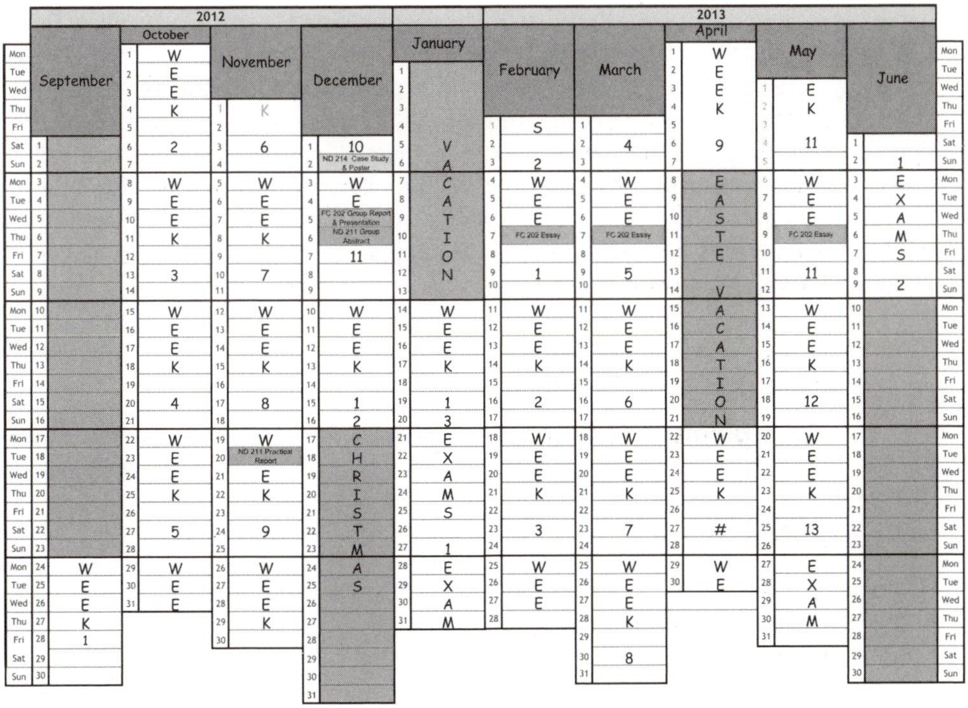

Figure 1.4   Year planner – 2012–2013

case study

I was first diagnosed with dyslexia and dyspraxia in 2008 a few months after enrolling on a BA (Hons) programme in Drama and Applied Theatre in Education. I am a mature student and had struggled at school with planning and organising my written work and with general time management. After several consultations with a dyslexia tutor, I became aware of how my learning difficulties were impacting upon my well-being as well as affecting my work. My tutor encouraged me to recognise my difficulties and explore organisational strategies to overcome these. I realised my stress was caused by the lack of a clear overview of the structure of the semester and assignment deadlines.

As a result, with the encouragement of my tutor, I experimented with various strategies and the use of technology and software. The first important step was to create a colour coded assignment list using MS Word so that I could visualise at a glance what objectives and deadlines I had to meet over the forthcoming year. I kept this on my wall as a reminder and motivation tool. I also created a weekly timetable using Google Calendar, visually identifying my lectures, seminars, individual study time and assessment dates, including time for relaxation and exercise. I was able to access and edit my calendar using my Android Smart Phone, which also sent me reminders. As I could now see my time visually, I was able to plan my individual study time with the use of a prioritised weekly to-do list. It was very satisfying to cross tasks off my list as they were completed and to reward myself for achieving my goals.

Being aware, and taking active control of my organisation has greatly reduced my stress. I no longer find myself rushing my work the night before to meet the deadline. Consequently, my time is much more structured. I can plan, write, proofread and edit my work using my assistive technology and still have time for relaxation and exercise! My confidence has grown, which is reflected in my enjoyment of the work and my grades. I am currently on course to achieve an upper 2:1 and am feeling confident about achieving my long-term goals.

points to remember

This chapter has introduced you to:

- self-esteem, managing well-being and maintaining motivation
- methods of planning and organising your workload
- meeting deadlines
- planners, weekly timetables and 'to do' lists
- useful new technologies and software for organisation.

CD-ROM Contents

Please go to the CD-ROM accompanying this book to find the following documents:

Activity Log Example	Word Document
Activity Log Template	Word Document
Blank Weekly Planner	Excel Template
Colour Coded Assignment List Example	Word Document
Course Benefits Template	Word Document
Firefox and Delicious Guide	Word Document
Google Calendar Guide	Word Document
Managing Challenges Example	Word Document
Managing Challenges Template	Word Document
Prioritised To Do List Guide and Example	Word Document
Prioritised To Do List Template	Word Document
SMART Goals Example	Word Document
SMART Goals Template	Word Document
Task Breakdown Example – Organising My Notes	Word Document
Task Breakdown Template	Word Document
To Do List	Word Document
Urgent/Important Guide	Word Document
Using Dropbox	Word Document
Using New Technologies and Software Information and Guides	Word Document
Weekly Planner First Example	Excel Document
Weekly Planner Second Example	Excel Document
Weekly Planner Semester 1 First Example	Word Document
Weekly Planner Semester 1 Second Example	Word Document
Weekly Planner Template (Excel)	Excel Document
Weekly Planner Template (Excel) Instructions	Word Document
Weekly Planner Template (Word)	Word Document
Weekly Planner Template (Word) Instructions	Word Document
Well-being and Mindfulness Information	Word Document
Year Planner (Baseline)	Excel Template
Year Planner 2012 to 2013	Excel Template

Please go to the CD-ROM accompanying this book to find links to the following:

Mind Tools – Time Management
Virginia Tech Study Skills

2

Understanding Your Preferred Learning Style

Sandra Hargreaves and Paula Baty

developmental objectives

This chapter:

- gives an overview of the concepts of thinking and learning styles
- allows you to reflect on how you currently think and learn
- presents strategies to help you to improve your methods and become a more effective learner
- provides a learning styles questionnaire to help you find out how you learn best (see link on the CD-ROM)
- explores a range of strategies and techniques associated with the main learning styles – auditory, visual and kinaesthetic.

A lot has been written about **thinking (cognitive)** and **learning** styles and the aim of this chapter is to help you to find out how you learn most effectively and to try other ways of learning that you may find helpful. Remember you don't have to do everything the same way. As Peri (one of the authors of Chapter 4), has often said, 'I don't make toast the same way I get five dogs in the back of the car'. The key is to make the most of your strengths and minimise your weaknesses.

Thinking styles

Some people know instinctively that they are **holistic** or **analytical** thinkers. If you are a **holistic** thinker, you prefer to think about a **whole** theme, idea or topic before breaking it down into its constituent parts. Another way of describing this way of thinking is '**top down**'. If you are analytical, you prefer to conceptualise in smaller, sequential stages, building the big picture from the '**bottom up**'. Some tasks are more suited to an overview approach and some require a more systematic sequential approach. For example, making a rough estimate on the basis of approximations is a holistic activity, whereas adding up a column of numbers is an analytical activity.

When discussing approaches to mathematics (see Chapter 9) the terminology changes, describing approaches as those of '**grasshoppers**' referring to holistic thinkers and '**inchworms**' referring to analytical thinkers (Chinn and Ashcroft, 1998).

In Figure 2.1 the vertical axis indicates the thinking style spectrum. The more analytical you are (the more you think first of detail), the higher up on this axis you are. Conversely, the more holistic you are (the more you think of the big picture), the lower down you are. No one is likely to be wholly one or the other. The horizontal axis shows the range of how we think: from thinking in words (verbalising) to thinking in images (visualising). Many people use both thinking processes and comfortably move from one to the other.

You can plot how you think you learn onto this graph. I, for example, know that I am a holistic verbaliser so that I learn best by looking at the whole

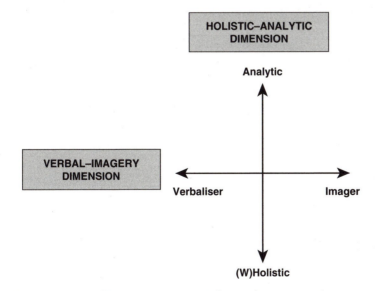

Figure 2.1   Cognitive styles and learning strategies (Riding and Rayner, 1998)

concept or topic before breaking it into smaller components and I also learn best by articulating my thoughts. Try to plot where you think you lie on this diagram.

Learning styles

So far as learning styles are concerned some students know that they learn better through **visual** methods and that they cannot absorb material when it is only delivered in auditory form such as through a lecture or on tape. Others prefer **auditory** input as they find visual processing difficult. Another group may find that they only learn if they process material while moving, making a model or drawing a plan, which is **kinaesthetic**. There are many overlaps in all these strategies; for example, drawing or creating a concept map is both visual and kinaesthetic. It is also unusual and not good practice for lectures to be totally auditory. Good lecturers include visual elements such as PowerPoint projections and illustrations to break up their delivery. Interactive question and answer sessions and role-play situations involve both auditory and kinaesthetic strategies. There is a wide variety of auditory, visual and kinaesthetic strategies, which are explained in this chapter.

If you feel that you know what your learning style is, look at the strategies below, which are suggested under the headings for visual, auditory and kinaesthetic. If not, you might like to do the internet **questionnaire** (see link on the CD-ROM) to see if it helps you to understand what strategies you use. Note that this link is only one of many different questionnaires attempting to identify learning style.

(GO to VARK – A Guide to Learning Styles on CD-ROM)

When reflecting on how you learn best, along with thinking and learning style, you might also like to take the following factors into consideration:

- motivation
- environment
- physiology
- time.

Refer to the How Do I Learn Best Concept Map on the CD-ROM to think about how you might learn more effectively.

Learning strategies

Strategies and techniques are provided in both bullet point format and in a concept map. As you will see from the examples provided below, many of the strategies and techniques do not suit just one learning style, but are in fact multi-sensory.

Visual

There are many strategies a visual learner can employ to aid learning and recall (see Figure 2.2). Visual imagery and association can play an important part.

The following list covers many visual strategies:

- Try making up **posters** to display around the room, using pictures to link with words or represent particular aspects of a topic. Use **bright colours** and **colour code** different sections, and use large **font** to make the layout clear and eye-catching.
- **Concept maps** or Mind Maps™ (Buzan) are particularly useful for brainstorming, essay planning, and exam revision. You could draw them onto posters, or use mind-mapping (Buzan) software such as Inspiration, Mind Manager and Mind Genius. (Note: the term Mind Map™ was created by Tony Buzan and the idea has been used in many software programs such as those listed above. For more information see *The Mind Map Book* by Tony Buzan with Barry Buzan, 2006.)
- Use **rooms** in your house for different subjects. For example, in your kitchen, place post-it notes on different appliances and objects to associate them with particular topics. Your **toaster**, **fridge** and **microwave** could all represent different aspects of material you are trying to learn. Then when you are trying to recall the information elsewhere, visualise yourself in your kitchen to trigger your memory.
- Using **visual memory pegs** is another method of recalling information. I have seen this method used very effectively in a wide range of tutorials but it is important to choose your own visual pegs to represent the numbers in the list so that you can recall them easily and link them effectively to what you are trying to learn. The original idea for this can be found in Buzan (1988) *Make the Most of Your Mind*, but has been adapted to suit personal visual cues. Figure 2.3 shows how the numbers from 1 to 10 can be linked to a visual image, which looks like the number. These visual images can then be linked to whatever you are trying to recall.
- When **revising** for exams, you could write questions with answers on the back of index cards. It is a good idea to **colour code** your **index cards** so that you have different coloured cards for each subject or topic (see Chapter 10, 'Examination Techniques').
- **Planners** or **wall charts** are visual and are a good way of organising and planning your workload (see Chapter 1, 'Managing Your Workload'). Enter onto them all your coursework deadlines and examination dates, as well as any important social events or activities. Monthly, semester or even yearly planners allow you to have an overview of important deadlines and events, allowing you to plan in advance. Weekly planners can help you to organise your workload on a day-to-day basis. Use a different coloured **highlighter** pen for each subject, or regular activity, such as a yoga class. Planners can be enlarged and put onto your wall to jog your memory, help you keep on task and to keep appointments on time. They can also be used as screen savers.

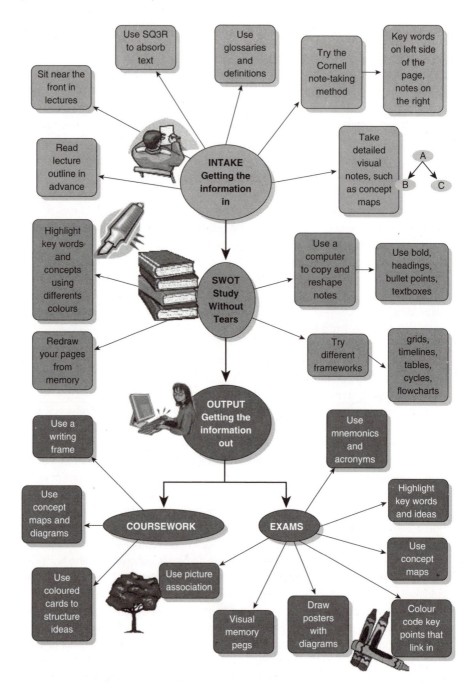

Figure 2.2 Visual learning strategies

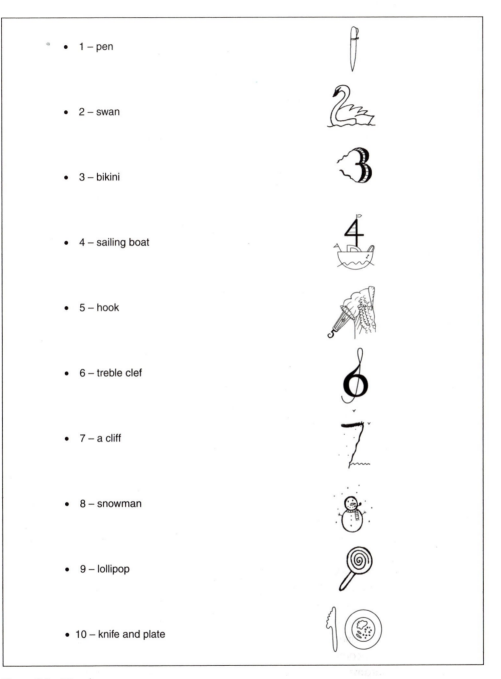

- 1 – pen
- 2 – swan
- 3 – bikini
- 4 – sailing boat
- 5 – hook
- 6 – treble clef
- 7 – a cliff
- 8 – snowman
- 9 – lollipop
- 10 – knife and plate

Figure 2.3   Visual memory pegs

Auditory

There are many strategies an auditory learner can employ to aid learning and recall (see Figure 2.4). **Sound imagery** and **association** can play an important part. The following list covers many auditory strategies:

- **Mnemonics** are auditory devices, such or rhymes or catchy phrases, which act as important aids to recall information, for instance factual terms and material or even how to spell a word. An example of this is the phrase 'there is a **rat** in sepa**rat**e', to remind you how to spell this word. Many music students remember the notes, which represent the lines and spaces of the treble and bass clefs, through mnemonics. The notes **EGBDF**, which represent the lines of the treble clef, are usually remembered with the mnemonic: **E**very **G**ood **B**oy **D**eserves **F**ruit.

- **Acronyms** are very common auditory devices which use the first letter of each key word to make a new word, for example: **WHO** for **W**orld **H**ealth **O**rganization and **UNESCO** for **U**nited **N**ations **E**ducational, **S**cientific and **C**ultural **O**rganization. Many of these have become so embedded in the structure of the language that they have become words in their own right. You can use this technique to help you remember information for examinations, as you will see in Chapter 10, 'Examination Techniques'. The word doesn't have to be a real word; it can be something which you have made up – which may even make it more memorable to you. Applying a rhythm or a beat to it can also help you to remember it.

- Sound imagery and association are used in **auditory memory pegs** for those who prefer to learn by auditory methods. This very useful memory device is set out in Tony Buzan's excellent book on memory, *Use Your Head* (1995). The auditory memory pegs are based on the old English rhyme This Old Man and each number in the rhyme is **linked to a word which sounds like the number**. The old rhyme goes:

    This old man, he played one, he played knick-knack on my drum

    and continues through all the numbers: two/**shoe**, three/**knee**, four/**door**, five/**hive**, six/**sticks**, seven/**heaven**, eight/**gate**, nine/**wine** and ten/**hen**. As with the visual pegs it is important to know these auditory pegs well, and to be able to recall them immediately. Thus when you have linked them in memory with whatever information you are trying to remember, your recall of the information will be improved. (For further information on this technique with excellent illustrations, see *Use Your Head* by Tony Buzan.)

- Try **reading your work aloud**, or getting someone else to read it aloud for you. Many people find that by using this technique, they are able to hear how their work sounds, in order to spot any mistakes and then make corrections. Mistakes are often difficult to spot when you have read it over many times to yourself. Reading aloud also allows you to check your punctuation. This way you can pick up on natural pauses where it may be necessary to add commas or full stops.

- **Software programs**, such as TextHELP Read&Write, ClaroRead, SpeakQ and Kurzweil **can also read back your work to you**. If you are having trouble reading difficult text or challenging articles, you can also scan in pages of text or articles, which can be read back to you using the software.

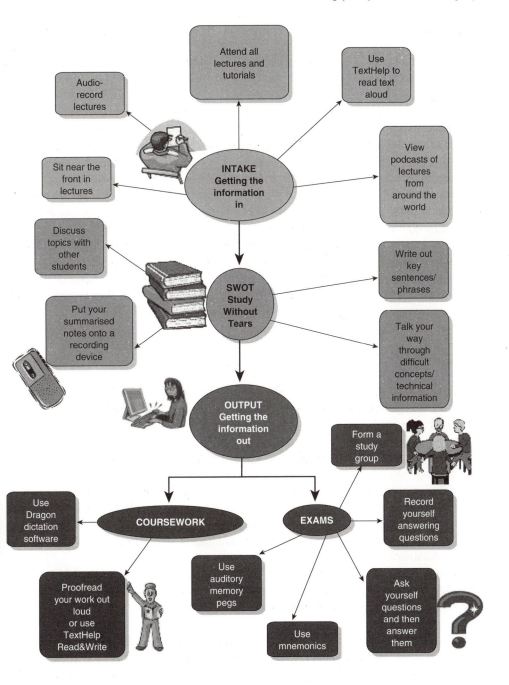

Figure 2.4   Auditory learning strategies

- If you have difficulty word processing but no difficulty articulating your ideas, you might benefit from using another software program, Dragon Naturally Speaking, and other similar packages, which **convert your speech into text** files. This software needs to be trained but is used widely by both dyslexic and non-dyslexic people who find it very helpful to write essays, reports and emails.
- If you find it difficult to take notes in lectures, and often find that you are not able to take down enough information, you could try using a mini-disk recorder or other recording device to **record your lectures so that you can listen to them later** at home at your own pace. All you need to do during the lecture is write down the number on the elapsed time counter at significant points in the lecture. Then at home, and as soon as possible, use the counter to fast forward to selected sections and **make notes on the content** (see Chapter 3). The actual recording can be used for revision but be aware this could become time consuming. Be selective!
- A useful way of developing your understanding of a subject or concept is to **talk it over with someone**. You could get together with a classmate and discuss ideas with them, which of course will help them too. If you are unsure of what an essay question is asking you to do, discuss what your understanding is of the question with your lecturer or module tutor so that you can ensure you are on the right track.

Kinaesthetic

Some kinaesthetic learners find they study best while **moving, listening** to music, or **chewing** gum or **eating** something. Further suggestions are provided in Figure 2.5 and below.

- You could compile **study notes** on a mini-disk and listen to them while going for a walk or a jog.
- If you are revising for exams, you may find it helpful to write out your notes a few times, condensing them down to just a few **key words** that will trigger your memory of the subject. You could use highlighter pens to colour code different topics, or draw pictures to relate to the different topics (see Chapter 10, 'Examination Techniques').
- If you enjoy a hands-on approach, you may like to experiment with plastic letters or modelling letters in clay to learn words and letters you find difficult. An effective multi-sensory spelling strategy is the **Look, Say, Cover, Write, and Check** method, which is covered in Chapter 8.
- If you have a presentation to do, **practise your presentation** in front of someone you know, in the mirror or on video. This will help to build your confidence and will allow you to check that you have got the timing right. If the presentation is meant to be for 15 minutes, make sure it is no longer and don't bore your audience by running over time. PowerPoint is a very useful tool for presentations for both dyslexic and non-dyslexic students as it helps you to speak articulately with prompts from the screen,

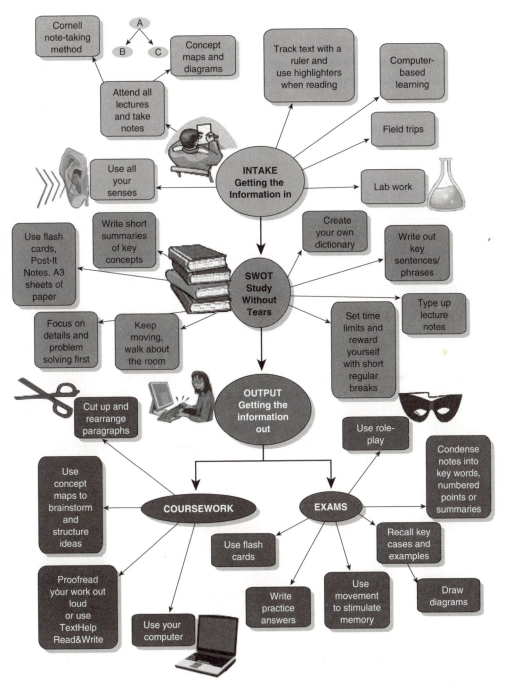

Figure 2.5   Kinaesthetic learning strategies

which you can move on with simple key-strokes. The other wonderful thing is that if you are nervous, the PowerPoint slides direct the audience's attention away from you to the screen.

- **Role play** is an effective way of putting your knowledge into practice. If you are training to be a nurse or teacher, for example, try role playing a consultation with a patient, or an interview with a parent (see Chapter 11, for further ideas).

case study

Doris, a psychology student, found this type of visual/kinaesthetic approach helpful because she could visualise all the ideas and issues involved before moving on to the outline of the essay and the essay itself (see Chapter 5, 'Answering Essay Questions').

Essay concept map

The key to this concept map is organisation by colour. By isolating the issues that need to be addressed in the brief in different colours I was able to see at a glance what I needed to cover and how the various issues were linked. The concept map also gave me the structure for the essay. The left of the concept map (the issues not related to an intervention) formed the basis of my introduction and how I was going to address the question. This delineated how I conceived the issues and the agencies I thought should be involved in the intervention. On the right-hand side of the concept map are those issues that are related to the proposed intervention. As you can see the issue of shift work is mentioned but no intervention is proposed. This is part of the job description and not possible to change; my reading, however, indicted that it was a significant risk factor and therefore should be mentioned in the write-up.

The Case Study Concept Map shown on the CD-ROM (see Figure 2.6) was produced by Doris in response to the following essay question on vocational health issues:

Gary Frost is a 49-year-old married father of two, who has worked shifts as a long distance lorry driver for the past 20 years. He spends most of his time in his cab, travelling across England. He finds his job isolating and quite stressful at times. He often becomes agitated and restless, feeling hostile towards other drivers on the road when spending long periods of time sitting in traffic on the motorway. He eats mainly fast, fatty foods whilst he is on the road and finds little time to exercise. Mr Frost smokes 30 cigarettes a day and has recently suffered with chest pains. His wife is becoming increasingly worried about his health, but Mr Frost thinks that his wife is worrying over nothing and that his recent chest pains are simply a result of indigestion caused by eating and driving simultaneously.

Identify and refine problems or issues related to this case. Identify the roles of a health psychologist and other health care professionals dealing with this case. Develop an appropriate treatment/intervention plan.

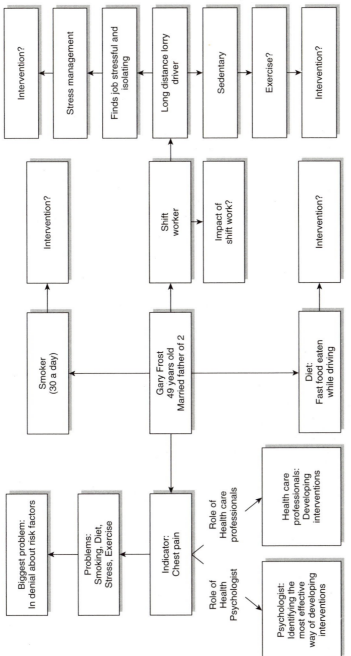

Figure 2.6   Case study concept map

points to remember

- Understand your thinking style (holistic or analytical) and your learning style (visual, auditory, kinaesthetic or multi-sensory).
- Try to use your own cognitive and learning styles to develop techniques that will help you.
- Be prepared to use multi-sensory methods and different methods for different purposes.
- Use materials or software that appeal to your own needs and be prepared to adapt them if necessary.
- Don't be surprised if you prefer to work in a range of methods and techniques – try them and use what is successful.
- Be prepared to seek or ask for more expert help if this is appropriate.

CD-ROM Contents

Please go to the CD-ROM accompanying this book to find the following documents:

Auditory Learning Strategies Concept Map	JPEG image
Case Study Concept Map	Word document
First-year Medical Students Prefer Multiple Learning Styles	PDF
How Do I Learn Best? Concept Map	Word document
Kinaesthetic Learning Strategies Concept Map	Word document
Visual Learning Strategies Concept Map	JPEG image
Visual/Verbal Learning Strategies Concept Map	Word document

Please go to the CD-ROM accompanying this book to find links to the following:

BBC Learning Styles
Kolb's Learning Styles
Learning Styles
VARK – A Guide to Learning Styles
Word Q + Speak Q

3

Note Taking and Note Making

Kay McEachran

developmental objectives

This chapter:

- considers the difficulties of note taking and note making
- illustrates the importance and purpose of good notes
- considers the role of learning style
- looks at various strategies for compiling notes
- analyses different systems for taking and making notes
- shows you how to make use of appropriate technology
- provides useful examples and templates for note taking and note making.

Difficulties

Note taking and note making at college or university can be especially difficult for dyslexic students, as both activities require you to perform a number of different tasks at once, some of which you may have difficulty with. These can include: listening comprehension; reading comprehension; information processing; organisation, flow and structuring of work; clarity of writing; and writing speed.

One area you may have particular difficulty with is knowing exactly what information to write down and what to leave out, which can result in you either desperately trying to note everything down or giving up entirely. **You don't need to write down everything that is said in a lecture**. If, for example, a lecturer tells a joke or an amusing anecdote, you must ask yourself if it is crucial to your understanding of the topic being discussed; if it isn't, then disregard it.

Identifying **key points** and the organisation and structure of notes can be problematic. Here, you can either take the lead from your lecturer, or the author if you are making notes from text. They will have done the bulk of the work for you – especially if your lecturer provides handouts. **Headings and subheadings indicate key points** and they will more than likely be given in a logical sequence. So make the most of the work already done for you.

You will not be the only student who is daunted by the prospect of taking or making notes. By introducing and practising useful strategies your notes will improve, hopefully making the process easier.

Differences between note taking and note making

Generally speaking, **note taking involves taking notes from speech (e.g. lectures, videos, audio tape, and dictation)** where there is less control of the process and usually more pressure because of time restrictions. Even when this exercise involves copying from a board or overhead projector, there tends to be a time limit.

Note making (usually from text or rewriting notes) is not subject to the same time constraints. Students often feel that they have more control when they are making notes and therefore tend to feel less pressured by this activity. Making notes enables you to reorganise your thoughts and ideas, and put them into your own words, rather than your lecturer's, and hopefully remember them better because of this.

The importance of good notes

This should not be underestimated. Your academic success will undoubtedly depend on the quality of your notes, as they will form the basis of your exam revision and essays or assignments. It is vitally important that you approach your note taking and note making seriously from the very beginning of your course. Try not to fall behind – you may not have time to catch up later on.

Good notes can be one of the most important resources for all students for both assignment preparation and examination revision. To appreciate this fact you will have to identify your reasons for taking/making them (their purpose), as well as their functions.

Why take or make notes?

- To engage/interact with the material being studied.
- To assist in writing essays and assignments.
- To formulate ideas.
- To remember and make sense of material.
- For revision purposes.
- For reviewing or reformulating ideas.

The importance of identifying learning style

The value of identifying your learning style lies in **helping you identify your strengths and weaknesses**, and might therefore encourage you to concentrate on using strategies which complement your areas of strength when compiling notes.

If you are a **visual learner**, you may have a preference for concept maps (for holistic thinkers) and linear notes (for analytical thinkers). You might also like to compile wall charts or diagrams and use colour. If you are an **auditory learner**, you may prefer to record lectures and/or yourself talking about the lecture afterwards. Other auditory approaches would be to discuss the lecture topic with friends or listen for **clues** and **signal words** during the lecture. Examples of these would be: 'an important theory is', 'the main points are', or statements like 'next we will consider'. **Kinaesthetic learners** prefer active learning and might like to use a combination of the methods above.

Listed below are a number of general strategies for note taking and note making, many of which are **multi-sensory** (i.e. appeal to all learning styles). It should be stressed, however, that these are only guidelines and that you should be flexible and use whichever strategies you feel comfortable with, regardless of your learning style.

Don't limit yourself to learning methods considered suitable for your learning style. Mix and match strategies to suit yourself. Chances are, you will know which methods work best for you anyway. **If one method is not working for you, try another**.

General strategies for note taking and note making

- Prepare in advance if possible and familiarise yourself with the topic. Keep ahead of your required reading by asking for a prioritised reading list which indicates the essential source material. This may help to ensure that you have more idea of those points which are worth noting down, and those which aren't, thereby giving you more time to listen. **Lectures will make more sense if you already have a general idea of what the lecturer is talking about**.

- Be **punctual and ready to take notes from the very beginning** of the lecture. This is when most lecturers will **provide signposts and key points**. Use these – if your lecturer has taken the trouble to mention them, they will be important.
- Listen to your lecturer's **summing up at the end of a lecture**, to ensure you have included all the points listed.
- Jot down key words and phrases.
- **Always attend class, if you can**. Second-hand notes are difficult to decipher. By all means use another student's notes in addition to your own, but you still need the gist of the lecture in order for them to be useful. Only use another's notes as a last resort.
- Use **a large loose-leaf notebook** (a different one for each module/subject). This way you can easily insert extra pages or remove pages in future.
- Write the date and title at the top of the first page – it makes filing easier.
- **Only write on one side of the paper**, double space the lines, and leave plenty of space (for adding points later).
- Write source references and page numbers in the margin.
- Follow the **book or chapter order** when making notes from text. This will ensure your notes follow a logical sequence.
- Leave out unnecessary words (such as the, a, an).
- Use **shorthand, abbreviations or symbols**, particularly for words common to your subject. You can design your own (the more personal the better).
- Use thought plans or Mind Maps™ as this may help you link ideas and concepts.
- Indicate the words you don't understand or have difficulty in spelling by highlighting them or writing them in a different **colour**. You could even just write them in **bold**, BLOCK CAPITALS or in larger print if you find this quicker or you don't have any colours with you.
- Have a **dictionary to hand** when making notes or rewriting notes, to check any unfamiliar words. **Do not do this when taking notes** – you will not have time!
- Copy the **information provided on boards or overheads**, as they will contain the points that your lecturer considers to be important. (Remember, they know what is necessary to pass your course!)
- Sit next to a good note taker – near point copying is often easier than copying from a board or overheads. (Remember, copying notes is not cheating, but do ask first!)
- Ask your lecturer to provide copies of **overheads and handouts** before the start of the lecture. If they are available electronically, download them in advance. This way you may only need to make additional notes or examples.
- **Record lectures** if you have difficulty taking notes, but remember to ask your lecturer. Auditory learners may find this a useful supplement to the notes they take in class.
- If your **keyboard skills are better** than your handwriting skills, **take a laptop to lectures**, or use a small keyboard and download onto your computer later. Always check beforehand if this is permissible.
- Write up notes as soon as possible after the lecture.
- Talk about the lecture with classmates afterwards and record the conversation.
- When making notes record any additional questions or ideas as they occur to you. They can be added later. This will not only prevent you from forgetting valuable points or topics to research but will also stop you becoming distracted and straying from the task at hand.

Not all of these strategies will be suitable for you. **Only use those that work for you in conjunction with one or more of the suggested techniques for compiling notes** (see below) in order for your notes to be as effective as possible.

Suggested note taking and note making methods

The Two Column Method (Cornell system)

(GO to Two Column (Cornell) Template and Example on CD-ROM)

This double entry system is considered particularly suitable for dyslexic students for two reasons:

- It applies to both note taking and note making.
- It is a multi-sensory technique requiring you to record, reduce, recite, reflect on, and review your notes.

The method follows three basic steps:

Step 1   Before the lecture draw a vertical line 6 cm from the left-hand side of your page. This is the **recall column**. To the right of this margin is the **note-taking column**.

Step 2   During the lecture record notes in the main column as fully and clearly as you can. Use abbreviations – it will save time. Skip lines. You can do this for a number of reasons:

- To show the end of particular ideas or thoughts.
- If you lose your train of thought.
- You cannot keep up with the lecturer.
- You don't fully understand what is being said.

In each case, mark the gap with a symbol or word to identify the reason for the blank space. Using words such as 'END' or a question mark will help. If you are recording the lecture and your voice recorder has a counting device then take a note of the number at the point where you encounter difficulties. Alternatively, make a note of the time and this will help guide you to the section of the recording you will need to check later.

Step 3   After the lecture **reduce** your notes by jotting down ideas and **key words** (cues) in the recall column (use drawings and symbols if you prefer). These should immediately give you the idea of the lecture. This process should help clarify the meaning and relationships of ideas.

Next, recite the main facts and ideas of the lecture by covering the main column, and only using the cues in the recall column. This process helps commit facts and ideas to your long-term memory. At this stage you may also begin to reflect and come up with new ideas and relationships.

31

Finally, a quick **review** of the key words in your recall columns for a few minutes each week will help you remember much of what you have made notes on.

This method has many similarities to the SQ3R Reading Strategy discussed in Chapter 4 (pp. 42–43).

Advantages ✓	Interactive and extremely efficient once mastered – helps avoid rewriting notes.
Disadvantages ✗	You may need time and practice to get the hang of this method.

Q Notes (Question and Answer Notes)

(GO to Q Notes Template and Example on CD-ROM)

The originator (Jim Burke, www.englishcompanion.com) of this note-making system calls it Q Notes, because it requires that you make up Q-uestions (left-hand column), and Q-uiz yourself (right-hand answer column). **This process will no doubt be easier if you originally used the two-column method to compile your notes.**

For revision purposes cover up the answer column and look at the questions – these act as cues to remind you of what you should know.

Advantages ✓	An excellent revision aid.
Disadvantages ✗	As with the two-column method it may require practice.

Four Quarter Method

(GO to Four Quarter System Template and Example on CD-ROM)

You might find that dividing a page into 4 quarters helps with your note taking. Each of the quarters represents 15 minutes of an hour-long lecture (if your lecture is longer, say 2 hours, then you could divide up 2 pages).

Psychologically and visually this is a satisfying method, since you are always aware of just how far into a lecture you are. In addition, as space is limited, it encourages the use of **key words** and abbreviations. It is also a useful technique if you are recording a lecture, and do not have a counter on your recording device, as you will see at a glance which section/s of the lecture you have missed and should replay.

Advantages ✓	Encourages interactive note taking.
Disadvantages ✗	You will need to be very concise.

Linear

This method uses **subheadings, key points and lists** to highlight points. It may appeal more to visual learners. Figure 3.1 is an example of what brief linear revision notes on this chapter might look like, using a variety of these methods.

(GO to Linear Notes Example on CD-ROM)

Advantages ✓	May help keep you focused during lectures and keep with the flow of a lecture or argument. Can save you rewriting notes.
Disadvantages ✗	Very laborious. Can result in unnecessary material which you may be tempted to use simply because you have written it down. Only helps avoid rewriting notes if you are an efficient note taker in the first place. To be avoided if your handwriting speed is slow.

Concept maps (thought plans and spider diagrams)

Concept maps (as shown in Figure 3.2) begin with the main point/central theme written or drawn in the centre of the page. From this central idea or image a pattern of ideas are added via a series of connecting lines. These can represent ideas, themes, arguments, examples or relationships between ideas (e.g. cause and effect). These cross-links and cross-references are easy to add and the expansion of ideas just continues outwards. Examples of Mind Maps™ can be found in Chapters 2 and 5.

By the nature of their design, concept maps can include **colours, drawings and symbols**. By using these maps, you can fit a whole lecture or topic onto one page (it is best to turn the paper horizontally).

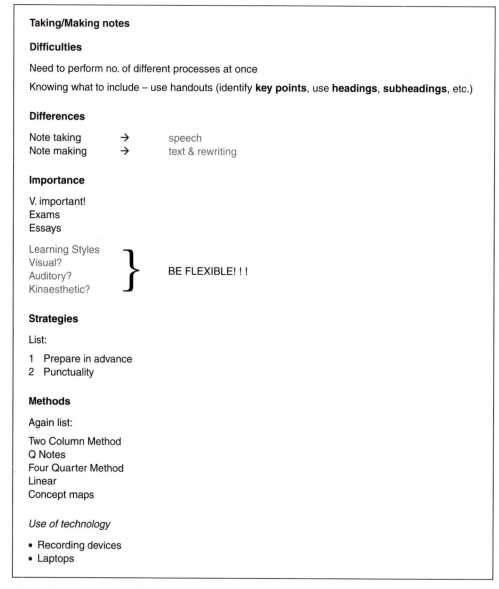

Taking/Making notes

Difficulties

Need to perform no. of different processes at once

Knowing what to include – use handouts (identify **key points**, use **headings**, **subheadings**, etc.)

Differences

Note taking	→	speech
Note making	→	text & rewriting

Importance

V. important!
Exams
Essays

Learning Styles
Visual?
Auditory?   } BE FLEXIBLE! ! !
Kinaesthetic?

Strategies

List:

1 Prepare in advance
2 Punctuality

Methods

Again list:

Two Column Method
Q Notes
Four Quarter Method
Linear
Concept maps

Use of technology

• Recording devices
• Laptops

Figure 3.1   An example of linear notes based on this chapter

Concept maps can be constructed by using pens and paper or by using software programs such as Inspiration or Mind Manager.

You might prefer using concept maps during lectures and converting them into more conventional linear notes afterwards.

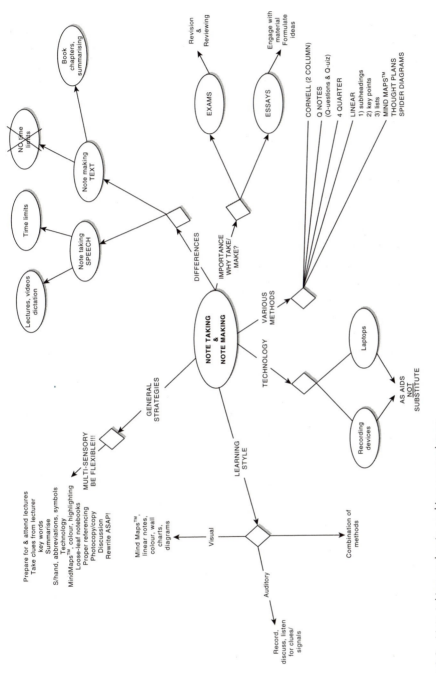

Figure 3.2   Note-taking and note-making concept map

Advantages ✓	Fewer words used. Useful if your handwriting speed is slow. They help organise and condense material.
Disadvantages ✗	Can be confusing and may require a certain amount of training. Must be organised systematically and consistently. More useful when making notes than taking notes.

Think of rewriting notes or converting them into concept maps or patterned notes as useful revision time. **Any activity that involves reprocessing notes improves recall** and therefore acts as a form of revision. In addition, you will be left with a set of understandable reusable notes for the future!

Recording notes

The use of recording devices and laptops for compiling notes can be a big help to the student with dyslexia. There are, however, some general points to be made and **advantages** and **potential pitfalls** to consider.

- Use **a recorder with a counting device**. If at some point you lose track, simply **make a note of the number on the counter**, then after the lecture you merely have to locate this number on the counter rather than listen to the whole lecture again.
- **Record yourself talking about a subject**, either following a lecture or when reading and making notes from text. This encourages the creative flow of ideas without the worry of having to write them down simultaneously – there will be time for that afterwards.
- **Label and date your recorded notes** in order to avoid confusion and make them easier to find.
- **Write up recordings as soon as possible** while they are still fresh in your mind. Be selective (see Chapter 2). As an alternative to writing up notes digital recorders can be used with Sonocent AudioNotetaker to manage your recordings.
- **Voice recorders** or even **mobile phones** can be used for this purpose, since many now have a facility for recording speech. Both devices are extremely useful as they fit easily into pockets and can therefore be ready to hand all of the time (e.g. when out walking, travelling to and from college or just going about your daily business).
- **Speech to text software**, such as Dragon Naturally Speaking (for PCs) or Dragon Dictate (for Macs) can also be extremely useful for making notes. Although you may have to train the software to recognise your voice it will certainly minimise the amount of writing or typing that you have to do and is particularly useful if you are better at articulating your thoughts and ideas verbally rather than in writing.

Advantages ✓	Very useful for students with an auditory preference, and/or a slow handwriting speed.
Potential pitfalls ✗	Try only to use this method as a back-up, as you may become a passive rather than an attentive listener and/or end up with a backlog of recordings. Remember, compiling notes should be an **interactive experience**.

Using laptops, netbooks and tablets

Taking a laptop, netbook, small keyboard or tablet computer into lectures can be very useful if you have good keyboard skills. If you can touch type, then you will be able to concentrate on the board, or overheads without having to keep looking down at what you are writing.

Advantages ✓	Your notes will be legible, and easy to expand upon at some point in the future, thus saving time. You are able to use the spellchecker or thesaurus on your PC.
Potential pitfalls ✗	Don't neglect your handwriting skills. Always ask permission to use a keyboard. Don't take your spellchecker for granted – they are useful, but not infallible.

Technology should be used as an aid when compiling notes, **but never as a substitute** for your own notes.

case study

Atif had a written test, which was unusual for his course as most of it was based on course work, much of it practical. He worked on making revision notes. He knew which topics were likely to come up in the test, but his lecture notes weren't really up to scratch. He did have his course handouts, however, which we worked through to make notes on each of the major topics. He used the headings and subheadings as signposts. He had a visual preference, and by using a combination of drawings, colour, illustrations, Mind Maps™ and abbreviations he managed to fit each topic onto a single page. As well as now having notes for future use, the physical act of converting the lecture notes into an understandable and usable format caused him to review his notes and therefore acted as revision. He passed his test with a very good mark. He explained that once he had converted his course handouts into his own words and drawings the test was psychologically less of a challenge. It had seemed 'a much smaller hill to climb'. He was also less afraid of written tests in the future.

points to remember

This chapter has introduced you to:

- the importance of good note taking/making
- overall strategies to help with note taking and note making
- various note-taking and note-making methods
- the role of technology in compiling notes.

Remember – the beauty of taking or making notes is that you only have to please yourself. All that matters is that **your notes make sense to you**. Marks are not gained for the notes themselves, but rather your ability to **utilise them for revision or coursework**.

CD-ROM Contents

Please go to the CD-ROM accompanying this book to find the following documents:

Four Quarter System Example	Word Document
Four Quarter System Template	Word Document
Linear Notes Example	Word Document
Q Notes Example	Word Document
Q Notes Template	Word Document
Two Column (Cornell) Example	Word Document
Two Column (Cornell) Template	Word Document

Please go to the CD-ROM accompanying this book to find links to the following:

Dragon Naturally Speaking
English Companion
Sonocent AudioNotetaker

4

Reading Strategies and Speed Reading

Peri Batliwala and Judith Cattermole

developmental objectives

This chapter aims to help you:

- understand your present reading habits
- use your library
- apply an efficient reading strategy to your reading
- understand how comprehension can be enhanced
- understand how reading speed can be improved.

Reading at college or university

It is obvious but necessary to state that one of the greatest demands of college or university life for any student is the reading load, in terms of both quantity and complexity. There is some variation, depending on the course chosen, but it is fair to say that if you can't read efficiently and with reasonable fluency, you will feel overwhelmed and under-equipped for all the tasks required of you: undertaking research, writing essays, understanding lectures, and ultimately, sitting exams.

It is critical therefore that you, as an adult dyslexic student with reading difficulties, seek help with **prioritising texts on reading lists,** by asking your tutors which are the most essential texts and **learning any strategies that make it possible for you to read efficiently and with good understanding.**

Reading and dyslexia

It is fairly generally agreed that reading weakness is a fairly reliable sign of the 'distinctive balance of skills', as Gilroy and Miles characterise dyslexia (1996, p. 1). Indeed it is reading weakness which gives rise to the 'discrepancy definition' of dyslexia when there is a marked discrepancy between a reading score and age/IQ. In other words **reading is probably harder for you than for non-dyslexic students.**

It is very important to set aside **specific time slots** for reading in your weekly schedule (see Chapter 1) and to stick to them. This will help in two ways. First, it will keep you on schedule and avoid the temptation of 'doing it later'. Secondly, it will stop you reading for longer than you have allocated in a particular subject area. Most dyslexic students report that they 'sit for hours reading and that nothing goes in'. You need to avoid this and can do so by **adopting a reading strategy** and by **changing your activity** when you are **losing concentration.** Break up your reading into chunks of 30- or 45-minute slots. If you are losing concentration even with a reading strategy, use shorter slots. It is important to use your time effectively and eliminate the feeling of despair which arises when you have spent hours in the library and feel you have learnt little.

Using a library

The library is an important source of help as it provides information and services as well as books, journals and other materials. It is important for you as a dyslexic student to take some time to explore the library before you need to start using it.

Start finding out about your library:

- By visiting and walking round. **Get to know where different things are located** before you need to find the materials you require. Often dyslexic students find it difficult to work in open plan spaces so ask if there are any small, quiet rooms or study carrels (individual desks with sides) that you can use to study in to avoid distractions. Take time to try out different desks or tables and choose the ones that suit you best. Sometimes the library can get very busy, so if this bothers you, **try to visit at quieter times** and when staff will have more time to help you.

- By visiting the library website. This will give you a summary of all the services on offer and probably a list of the names and contact details of staff who can help you.
- By contacting key members of the library staff. Some libraries have staff who have a special responsibility for helping students with dyslexia and other disabilities.

To help you use the library efficiently you will need to find answers to the following questions:

- How do you join the library?
- How many items can you borrow?
- What sort of library materials can you not take out? These are usually called reference materials and often include journals.
- Can you reserve books and how do you collect them?
- Are there any **special arrangements for dyslexic students**? These can include being allowed to borrow items for longer or not having to pay fines. Each library is different and sometimes issue dyslexic students with a special card.
- Can you renew or make reservations online or by phone?
- Can you use your own laptop in the library?

The main types of materials you will find in a library are:

- **Books:** These are usually arranged on the shelves by subject. Each book is given a reference or class number. You can find this number by using the library catalogue. To do this you will need to know either the **author** or **title** or **subject**. **Make sure you have the correct spelling!** Most catalogues are computerised and the library will have terminals you can use as well as being able to access the catalogue online remotely, e.g. from home or where you work. Some class numbers can be long (often ten or more digits) so make sure you have pen and paper with you to write down the number before you go to the shelves.
- **Journals or periodicals or magazines and newspapers:** These are usually shelved alphabetically by title. Remember that if a title starts with the word 'The', you must ignore it when looking on the shelves. So, *The Labour Law Journal* would be in the 'L' section of the journals.
- **Abstracts and indexes:** These give brief details of journal articles. They may look difficult to use but are in fact quite easy although you may need to ask for some help to start you off.
- **Electronic information:** A lot of the material including journals and abstracts and indexes you will need to use is now available electronically. Athens is an Access Management System developed by Eduserv that simplifies access to the electronic resources your organisation has subscribed to. You need to ask your subject librarian about how to use and access Athens. When you have been given your password you will be able to use it independently.

41

Noting the source

When reading, the student is drawing upon the **ideas and research of others**, usually as source material for an assignment or examination. To avoid plagiarism (see Chapter 5 'Answering Essay Questions') it is imperative to acknowledge one's sources with a reference. Every time the student states a fact or makes an assertion, it should be supported with a reference to an original source. There is more on referencing in Chapter 5 but the first steps are taken when reading. When reading an academic piece always record (see Chapter 3 'Note Taking and Note Making') the following:

- Author's name and initials. If two or three authors note all their names and initials; if more than three just note the first.
- Date of publication.
- Title of book or paper.
- Edition.
- Place of publication.
- Publisher.
- If a journal also note down the journal name, volume, issue or part number and the first and last pages of the article.
- The page numbers of quotations taken from the text.

Using a reading strategy

The basic concept behind all reading strategies is that you should **read with a purpose** so that your mind does not wander, and so that all the time you are reading you are on task and no time is wasted. All strategies employ three different types of reading – namely, **skimming, scanning and reading for meaning**. **Skimming** requires you to look quickly over a piece of text to check for the main features; **scanning** requires you to look for something specific such as an answer to a question; while **reading for meaning** requires reading directed towards comprehending the text.

Some of the reliable and well-known strategies are:

- **SQ3R** Survey, Question, Read, Recall, and Review (cited in Ott, 1997, p. 182)
- **PASS** Preview, Ask and Answer Questions, Summarise and Synthesise (cited in McLoughlin, Leather and Stringer, 2003, p. 137).

To help you try one or more of these strategies we will look at the most well-known of these strategies, SQ3R, in more detail. The stages of the **SQ3R Method** are:

Survey	Look over the section or paragraph you are reading. This requires you to **skim read** to determine the length of the piece and if there are any subheadings or topic sentences you can then use for the next stage.
Question	If there are **subheadings** in the text, turn them into **questions** to give you a purpose for your reading. If there are no subheadings, look at the first sentence of each paragraph to see if it is a **topic sentence**. Change this into a question so that you can read the remainder of the paragraph to find the answer.
Read	This requires you to **read for meaning** so that you can answer the question you have raised in the previous step.
Recall	This stage ensures that you have understood the text you have read and can recall the information to answer the question you have raised. This may require you to **scan the text** for information such as a date or name.
Review	This final stage requires you to think about the information you have read and **to reflect** on whether you agree with it and whether it fits in with other reading you have done on the subject.

Additionally, there are often clues to content in the structure of many paragraphs. Therefore, it may be a good idea to focus on and absorb the topic sentence and concluding sentence of a paragraph, and develop a 'recognition span' for key words and phrases (Gilroy and Miles, 1996, p. 86).

(GO to SQ3R Reading Comprehension on CD-ROM)

PASS differs slightly from SQ3R. **Preview, Ask** and **Answer Questions** are similar to Survey, Question and Read, but with greater emphasis on answering questions as you read. The **Summarise** stage is Recall with note making (Chapter 3) and **Synthesise** implies reducing material as you analyse it and make notes.

Again whichever strategy you choose, the important thing is that you are **actively engaging with the material** to take what you need from it. **This puts you in control of your reading**.

Visual Stress (Scotopic Sensitivity/Meares-Irlen Syndrome)

This is a condition which affects some dyslexic students. If you have difficulty reading black typeface on white background, or you see 'rivers of white' running down the page, or the words become jumbled, you may have visual stress. Although you can follow this up with a formal assessment which will determine the colours that suit you, you can help yourself at very little cost. Go to a stationery shop and **try out some different coloured plastic folders**. Put in some black text on white paper and see which colour improves your ability to read and reduces your visual discomfort. You can use the same coloured background on your computer screen.

(GO to How to Change Windows 7 Background Colour on CD-ROM)

Sometimes Visual Stress assessments are funded by Student Finance England (SFE). For more information about the condition visit the Institute of Optometry website: www.ioo.org.uk/dyslexia.htm

Reading can be more difficult if the text is dense, full of jargon or abbreviations, and if it is poorly laid out. This could be due to a serif font (one with loops at the top and bottom of letters), small font size, poor spacing and right justification. Use a dictionary and thesaurus to clarify the words that are impeding your reading progress. The problems associated with layout can be rectified either by **photocopying and enlarging the text** and using coloured folders, or by **scanning the text into your computer**, and changing the font size and background to your preferred colours.

Ideal conditions for reading

Reading is easier if you are sitting in a comfortable, well-lit environment. Good posture optimises reading and comprehension. Sitting upright enables the brain to receive the maximum flow of air and blood, and means that lower back pain and shoulder aches are relieved. The brain 'sits up and pays attention' because the body is alert. Your eyes can make full use of their peripheral vision. Sit at a table in a relaxed, upright posture with the book on the table in front of you at a distance of about 50 cm.

What is comprehension?

To put it simply, there would be no point in reading if we didn't understand what the words meant.

To put it more technically, comprehension,

> when applied to **reading is an ability to understand and recall the contents of what has been read**. It requires fluent decoding skills (reading with automaticity), knowledge of word meanings and an ability to use previous experience or contextual cues to understand the meaning which is being conveyed by the words. (Ott, 1997, p. 376; emphasis added)

So if you can read faster, it doesn't mean that you will find it harder to understand what you are reading. On the contrary, dyslexia experts maintain that, 'being able to read quickly is … important to comprehension. Unless a person can read at a good rate they cannot keep the content in memory long enough to comprehend it' (McLoughlin et al., 2003, p. 62).

Efficient comprehension is the whole point of reading. At college or university, in the workplace, for practical purposes or for pleasurable good reading, **comprehension is the key skill**.

To spell it out, 'if one were to choose a particular aspect of reading which would predict success in an occupation it would be silent reading comprehension' (McLoughlin et al., 2003, p. 6).

The sort of comprehension required of you at college or university is **critical thinking**, i.e. making connections, identifying relevance, fitting new information into an existing framework or putting into context. It is not merely a matter of literal questioning which is reliant on short-term memory (like so many of the assessment methods in popular speed-reading books) but it is based more on inferential comprehension where you are expected to make connections, draw inferences, interpret, question and critically analyse a written text.

Speed reading

So if you think that your reading speed hinders your comprehension and could be improved, try some of the following techniques with a reading strategy. If you are too busy during term time, maybe try them in the holidays.

As a result of your diagnosis for dyslexia, you should be aware of your current reading speed. If not, it is worth asking your dyslexia coordinator for a reading test. You can do a rough reading test for yourself by reading an unfamiliar passage for 1 minute, then counting how many words you read. Or try the test on the internet: www.rocketreader.com/cgi-bin/portal/fun_tests/perception. The average speed for college/university students is between 200 and 250 words per minute (wpm).

What is important for you to know is that, whatever your speed, it can be improved with a combination of improved reading techniques to help you read faster, and a strategy to help you read more actively (i.e. knowing what it is you want from the text).

Techniques you can use to read faster

Theory 1	The eyes read by a series of jumps (saccades) and fixations (pauses) along the line of text. Fixations are the only times at which information is absorbed. These fixations can take between ¼ and 1½ seconds. Poor readers make frequent, longer fixations,

	fast readers fewer, shorter ones. Although we may have been told to read 'slowly and carefully' in the past, in the belief that we would understand more, in fact the opposite is true.
Technique	By **limiting the number of fixations** and making them quicker than usual, your eyes will move over the text more fluently, and with increased comprehension.
Theory 2	Poor readers read one word at a time. Actually our peripheral vision enables us to take in groups of words, up to 5–7 at a time, and to grasp the sense of the sentence.
Technique	**Move your eyes forward quickly, consciously forcing yourself to skim read words in clusters.**
Theory 3·	Poor readers often back-skip or regress because they haven't understood a word, or feel they have missed something, or because their attention has wandered. Regression means more fixations and more wasted time.
Technique	Consciously determine to **only move your eyes forward quickly**, to keep your attention on the page, and trust to your word knowledge and context to 'make up' for a word that you may have missed or not understood.
Theory 4	The eyes move more smoothly and efficiently if they are guided by a slim implement such as a pencil, chopstick or knitting needle. Moving your finger from word to word, on the other hand, slows down the reading while your hand on the page blocks your peripheral awareness of the surrounding text.
Technique	**Run a pencil or chopstick quickly and smoothly along the text** to guide your eyes forward line by line. Eventually just passing the pencil/chopstick down the page in a flowing movement will enable a real speed-reader to take in the chunks on either side at a glance.
Theory 5	While 'mouthing' the words you read may slow you down, sub-vocalisation (saying to yourself) or internal verbalisation is a vital part of learning to read and is necessary for understanding of content.
Technique	Try to push down any sub-vocalisation to a semi-conscious level so that it still aids comprehension, but doesn't interfere with rapid eye movement over the text.
Theory 6	Reading actively and with purpose, i.e. knowing what you want from a text, will enable faster and more efficient reading and comprehension.
Technique	SQ3R or PASS.

Faster reading and 'smarter' reading

You should practise all the techniques learnt above for different types of 'information-gathering' reading (i.e. not novels!). They will work better in conjunction with any helpful **reading strategy** that focuses on prediction, questioning and active reading, while skimming and scanning the material.

Putting it all together

Stage 1

Once you have read the theories explained above and understood the techniques, it is time for you to put them into practice.

The simplest way to do this is to start with a short piece of non-fiction text of average difficulty about a subject that you are interested in (for example, an article in a magazine or a newspaper article).

Use a **reading strategy** to survey how it is laid out and preview its contents. This will help you think about why you are reading a particular text and what information you are trying to extract from it.

When you are sitting comfortably, feeling alert and motivated then try putting the techniques into practice as you read the article.

Don't worry if you can't remember all of them or back-skip the occasional word, or whatever. Rome wasn't built in a day, as they say, and nor will you immediately unlearn years of inefficient reading habits.

But **with regular, sustained practice and motivation your reading speed will improve**.

At first you may feel that you didn't understand much of what you read as you were concentrating so hard on trying to remember the new techniques. But the more you practise and the more automatic the techniques become to you, the more your reading and comprehension will start to improve. **You have to trust** your cognitive abilities to make sense of what they read – the focused brain always tries to make sense of what it is presented with. It's a basic survival mechanism.

Stage 2

When you feel that your actual reading is faster and that you are using the techniques without thinking about them, then start evaluating your comprehension of the texts.

After a short, concentrated reading exercise, stop and:

1   Question yourself about the content.
2   Try paraphrasing what you have read as if you were explaining it to someone else. After all if you can't put it into your own words, you probably haven't understood it very well.

3   Try writing a brief summary of the main points of what you have read including as much detail as possible. Check this with the original text and see what you have missed out.

Note that this procedure can be associated with the SQ3R reading strategy where step 2 above corresponds to the 'recall' stage of the strategy and step 3 above corresponds to the 'review' stage of the strategy, and simply extended by making notes.

Stage 3

Soon you should feel ready to apply your newfound faster reading techniques on actual academic texts. Again, it is best to start off doing this for short, concentrated periods when you are feeling fresh and motivated.

Gradually you can start to extend these reading sessions, from a few paragraphs to a section, from a section to a chapter. **Eventually you will find that you are able to 'click' into this accelerated way of reading for a longer period without fatigue and with concomitant accelerated comprehension.**

Again keep checking your comprehension: what were the main points of what you read, what were the less important points, what were the peripheral details?

Using text readers

Text-to-Speech software packages can be of great help to students with dyslexia by converting digital text into an audio stream. Depending on the package the text can be in MS Word and PDF documents, on websites or in emails. As the text is read it is highlighted on the screen helping users recognise the word being spoken.

The key is to have the text in electronic format. In most universities, lecture notes, study guides and assignment briefs are available electronically on a web-based service such as Blackboard and Weblearn. If this is not available ask your tutors to provide the source files of presentations, lecture notes and handouts. If the electronic sources are unavailable to you, optical character reader (OCR) software packages and a scanner will convert analogue material (books, papers, journals) to digital files. Unfortunately this process can be time-consuming and is not 100% accurate. If OCR software is not supplied with your scanner a number of free software packages exist.

(GO to Free OCR Software on CD-ROM)

Some of the best commercial text-to-speech software packages are:

Read&Write 10 GOLD	http://www.texthelp.com/page.asp?pg_id=1263
ClaroRead	http://www.clarosoftware.com/index.php?cPath=355
WordQ and SpeakQ	http://www.goqsoftware.com/uk/

In addition there are a number of satisfactory free text-to-speech packages.

(GO to Free Text-to-Speech Software on CD-ROM)

Reading and the Kindle

The Kindle is a reasonably new digital device specifically for reading. It differs from other devices such as phones and computers in that it is not back-lit which makes the reading experience qualitatively different. There is a suggestion that the quality of the type makes it easier to read than conventional books or back-lit devices such as computers or phones. It is possible to change the font, line spacing and words per line, all of which can aid the dyslexic reader. It also has a read back function that, if enabled on the book you are reading, will allow you to hear how unfamiliar words sound. It also has a dictionary which will allow you to look up the meaning of words while you are reading. At present you are able to download books, magazines and newspapers.

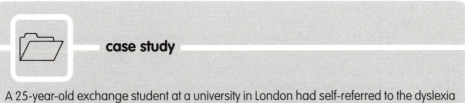

case study

A 25-year-old exchange student at a university in London had self-referred to the dyslexia department as he found he was struggling with the reading load of his course in geography. Not surprisingly, an assessment for extra exam time before Christmas revealed that his overriding weakness was reading speed, at 91 wpm for oral reading and 127 wpm for silent reading. Clearly if his reading speed could be improved, many of the problems he reported, such as poor concentration, an inability to keep up with the work, and patchy comprehension, would be improved too.

(Continued)

(Continued)

Over the next 8 weeks he worked with his tutor on a programme designed to address his slow reading; he was introduced to the theories behind how we read and the techniques needed to be a smart reader, as well as learning SQ3R. For him, this programme meant re-educating reading habits he had practised since boyhood. As he noted in an email following his initial assessment, 'I didn't really get the context straight away because I put so much effort into the reading process'. He was using all his efforts in the mechanical task of reading, so there was little left for memory or cognitive interaction. At week 5 he achieved his highest reading score of 495 wpm with high comprehension, when he was reading about a topic he was really interested in, but this fluctuated over the next 2 sessions to below 400 wpm. What seemed sensible for this student was to aim at achieving and maintaining a comfortable reading speed of around 350–400 wpm together with a 'smart' reading strategy like SQ3R. If he worked at this, it would not only help him overcome his difficulties at university, but also prove invaluable for his professional life.

Quick summary for learning to read faster and understand more

- Keep your eyes on the page – don't let them stray!
- Be active when you read – question what you want to find out and think about what you know about it already. SQ3R is a simple and effective strategy to help with this.
- Resolve to only move forwards – don't back-skip even if you don't understand a particular word or have missed a word.
- Don't mouth the words but sub-vocalise them to enhance the 'thought stream' of words in your head.
- Use a pencil or chopstick or knitting needle to guide your eyes quickly forward across the page.
- It is better to read fast for short periods – a chapter of a book, a section of an article – than to lose concentration trying to read over a longer period.
- Sit upright in a chair that supports your back with the text on a desk in front of you.
- Practising fast reading regularly will improve your speed and with it your levels of comprehension.
- Motivation is everything. You CAN improve your reading speed and comprehension if you decide to work on it.

 **points to remember**

- It is not important for you (or most of us) to aim to read faster and faster. Your aim should be to achieve and maintain a comfortable, efficient speed that serves your professional and personal needs, with good comprehension.
- As McLoughlin et al. soundly observe, 'Good readers vary their reading rate and comprehension level as a function of materials being read' (2003, p. 63) and also significantly, 'A good reader uses meta-cognitive skills in reading, is aware of the purpose of reading and differentiates between task demands' (2003, p. 63).
- Cottrell (2003, p. 125) makes the same point and provides examples of particular types of text for which slower reading may be more appropriate.
- Finally it is worth observing that, as with any self-help system, how much you achieve will depend on how much you put in. If you work at trying to read faster, and keep self-evaluating, before long you will see results. It is about trusting yourself, having confidence that you can improve, and wanting to.

CD-ROM Contents

Please go to the CD-ROM accompanying this book to find the following documents:

Conceptions of Privacy	PowerPoint Presentation
How to Avoid Plagiarism – Anglia Ruskin University	PDF
How to Change Windows 7 Background Colour	Word Document
SQ3R Reading Comprehension	Word Document

Please go to the CD-ROM accompanying this book to find links to the following:

ABC Study Guide Index Reading
Aquinas College Reading Clinic
Avoiding Plagiarism Tutorial
Doing Research
Free OCR Software
Free Text-to-Speech Software
MindTools Speed Reading
PlagiarismdotORG
TextHELP Systems

5

Answering Essay Questions

Sandra Hargreaves

developmental objectives

This chapter outlines the main stages in planning essays:

- 'unpacking the question'
- brainstorming or mind mapping to put down everything you can think of about the topic
- writing a theme for your essay to give you direction
- organising your brain storm or Mind Map™ into a sequential plan
- writing the essay in workable 'chunks'.

How often have you left your essay writing until the last moment and greatly regretted it? You're not the only one. Read the following case study and see what you can do to change your approach.

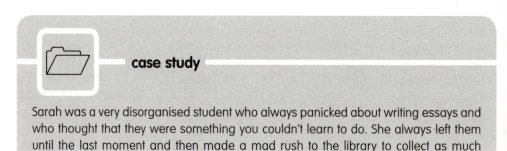

case study

Sarah was a very disorganised student who always panicked about writing essays and who thought that they were something you couldn't learn to do. She always left them until the last moment and then made a mad rush to the library to collect as much information as she could and often sat up all night writing the essay before handing it in the next day. Essays meant stress and exhaustion. When she discovered that they could be approached systematically she was surprised but willing to try the approach. After several attempts to write essays in this way she was amazed at the difference in both her own personal well-being and the quality of the essays. She now uses a run-up period of about six weeks to write major essays and goes through the steps: type of question, type of answer, key words, general issues and theme before moving on to the essay plan, the research and the essay itself. She organises the essay into manageable sections ('chunks') for writing. She also finds that she now has time to reread and edit her work after leaving it for a few days. Her marks have improved dramatically and she is no longer upset and stressed at the prospect of writing an essay. She is now so familiar with the technique that she can use it in examinations to prepare essays quickly and thoroughly. She also feels more confident that she has 'answered the question' as she has analysed it so carefully.

Unpacking the question

The first thing you must do is to **make sure that you understand the question**. Many dyslexic students have come to grief in essays and examinations by not reading or interpreting the question properly. Sometimes words are not understood and therefore a different interpretation is given. If you don't know what a word means, **look it up in the dictionary**. If you don't understand specific terminology, **go to your textbooks or ask your subject tutor**.

Make sure you read the instructions which come with the assignment. At this stage you need to ensure what areas need to be covered and what expertise is expected of you. As you progress through your course critical thinking will become more important. This is why it so important to analyse the question very carefully.

Analysing the type of question asked

It is essential to spend time on this stage of the essay. Table 5.1 has a list of **commonly used instruction words** with a definition or explanation of what they mean to make things easier for you. I first encountered it when teaching essay-writing skills in Sydney many years ago, but I haven't found anything better and many students find it helpful.

This list is not exhaustive. Can you think of **any other instruction words** and if so, what kinds of demands are made by them?

Table 5.1   Commonly used instruction words in essay questions

ACCOUNT FOR		give an **explanation** as to why.
ANALYSE	(1)	**examine** closely, break the subject up into the main ideas of which it is composed.
	(2)	**examine** a subject in terms of its components and show how they interrelate.
COMPARE		discuss the similarities and differences of two or more subjects, theories, etc., **stressing the similarities**.
CONTRAST		discuss two or more subjects, **emphasising their differences**.
DEFINE	(1)	**explain** (make clear) what is meant by.
	(2)	use a **definition** or definitions to explore the concept of, or state the terms of reference of.
DESCRIBE		present an **account** of, show that you understand the topic by writing about it in clear, concise English.
DISCUSS	(1)	investigate a subject, present an account of.
	(2)	consider and offer some **interpretation or evaluation** of.
ENUMERATE		give a **listing** or item by item account of.
EVALUATE		attempt to form a **judgement** about, appraise the clarity, validity or truth of a statement or argument against a set of criteria.
EXAMINE		**inspect** and **report** on in detail.
EXPLAIN	(1)	make clear the **details** of.
	(2)	show the **reason** for or underlying cause of, or the means by which.
ILLUSTRATE		offer an **example** or examples to:
	(1)	show how or that.
	(2)	show the reason for or underlying cause of, or the means by which.
INDICATE		focus **attention** on.
INTERPRET		set forth the meaning of; **explain** or elucidate.
JUSTIFY		show to be **just** and warranted.
LIST		same as **enumerate** – give an item by item account of.
OUTLINE		go through the **main features** of.
PROVE		show by **logical argument**.
RELATE	(1)	**tell**.
	(2)	bring into or **establish association**, connection or relation.
REVIEW	(1)	**report** the chief facts about.
	(2)	offer a **critique** of.
STATE		declare definitely or **specifically**.
SUMMARISE		describe in **brief** form.

Often questions are framed without explicit instruction words. They may be in the form of direct questions as follows:

- What is the minimal organisation for living organisms?
- What do you understand by the term 'money supply'?
- Why is Heathcliff such a destructive force in *Wuthering Heights*?
- How did medieval governments obtain the resources to govern?

The approach required by such questions can quite easily be seen by relating them to the implied instruction word. **What is/are** is like **outline** or **describe**, and calls for exposition of the main facts. **What do you understand by** is like **explain**, as are **how do/does/did. Why** is like **account for**.

While you are analysing the question you should be thinking of the type of answer the question calls for.

Planning your essay

Types of essays

There are basically five types of essay, which fall into two broad categories – namely, those which are intended to inform and those which are used to persuade. Notice how the types of essay outlined in Figure 5.1 correspond with the question types listed in the table above and noted at the end of each type.

An example of facing the question

Suppose you have been presented with the following question:

'Global warming is the greatest threat we face.' Discuss

- First, you should **analyse the question for what it is asking you to do**. It is basically an **evaluative question**, which requires you to give a judgement on the scale of the threat posed by global warming.
- Secondly, you should **decide what type of essay the question requires**. If you look at Figure 5.1 you will see that the essay falls into the 'writing to persuade' category and indeed requires an evaluative response. You need to think about the **criteria** you intend to set up to **evaluate** the threat, such as 'the greenhouse effect', rising temperatures, drought, food shortages and rising sea level, etc.
- Thirdly, you should **underline the key words** in the question as follows:

'<u>Global warming</u> is the <u>greatest threat</u> we face.' **<u>Discuss</u>**

- Fourthly, you should think about the major issues, which hang around the specifics of the question, and the larger context in which your discussion will be set. For example, what other threats do we face?

55

Writing to **Inform**	EXPOSITORY	**presents** established information in an **orderly manner**, either in classes, or in terms of a scale.
		OUTLINE, REVIEW (1), STATE, LIST, DESCRIBE
	EXPLANATORY	**accounts for** a phenomenon in the generally accepted way, showing how or why it happens (or happened), in terms of **interaction** within a system, or **cause and effect.**
		ACCOUNT FOR, ANALYSE (2), EXPLAIN (2)
Writing to **Persuade**	INTERPRETIVE	**presents** an individual **interpretation** of a body of data or literature, supported by a consistent set of **features** or **examples** from it. The interpretation is expressed in terms of a key word or phrase, or a classical model.
		DEFINE (2), DISCUSS (2), INTERPRET, RELATE
	EVALUATIVE	**presents** and justifies a **value judgement**, usually vested in a word of rather relative meaning (e.g. important, which needs to be linked up with certain clearly articulated criteria). The criteria normally imply scales against which individual cases may be ranked.
		EVALUATE, REVIEW (2), CRITICISE, DISCUSS (2)
	ARGUMENTATIVE	aims to **support a given proposition** by means of **logical reasons**, arguing their **validity**, and challenging the validity or relevance of any opposing arguments.
		PROVE, JUSTIFY

Figure 5.1   Definitions of essay types and instruction words which indicate their use

Brainstorming or mind mapping

The next stage in essay writing is to put down everything you can think of about the topic. This helps you to find out **what you already know** about the topic and **what you need to research**. A convenient way of doing this, especially if you are a **visual** learner, is to construct a **concept map**. Make sure you use lots of **colour**, as this helps you retain the images in your mind. This can be done with pens and paper (large sheets of A3 are the best) or by using a software program such as Inspiration or Mind Manager. These programs allow you to get your ideas down quickly (RapidFire in Inspiration), write notes and link to internet resources. When the concept map is complete and you are ready to start writing your essay the software allows you to see everything, including all your notes, sequentially and export the results into MS Word.

(GO to program shortcuts on CD-ROM)

Consider the essay question:

Has the **introduction** of **IT improved** the **way** we **communicate**? **Discuss**.

After following the steps suggested above you would have decided that the question is asking you to **explain** why you think the introduction of IT **has improved** the way we communicate, or conversely why it **has not improved** it. The question requires you to write an **interpretative** essay in which you would refer to **features** of communicating through IT and **examples** of it. You will have also underlined the key words to direct your attention to them.

The next stage is to **brainstorm** all your ideas into a Mind Map™ by hand or using software. Using Inspiration you may come up with something like Figure 5.2.

Writing a theme for your essay

This gives you **direction**, which will help you to stay on task and not wander off the topic. The theme can be expanded into the introduction and should cover what you are going to say in the essay.

Theme	There are many ways in which the introduction of IT has improved our methods of communication but overall the greatest improvement is the speed of that communication.
	OR
Theme	There are both advantages and disadvantages in our communication methods since the introduction of IT, but overall the advantages outweigh the disadvantages.

Note that there could be a variety of themes for this essay depending on your point of view.

Organising your brainstorm or Mind Map™ into a sequential plan

A **concept map can be changed into other formats** very easily, and then put into a **sequential plan or outline**, as illustrated below. The notes, which were made on each theme identified in a balloon in Figure 5.2 have appeared below each subheading in the outline. This was done on the Inspiration program. If this is to be done from a handwritten concept map, you will have to decide on the order that best illustrates your theme.

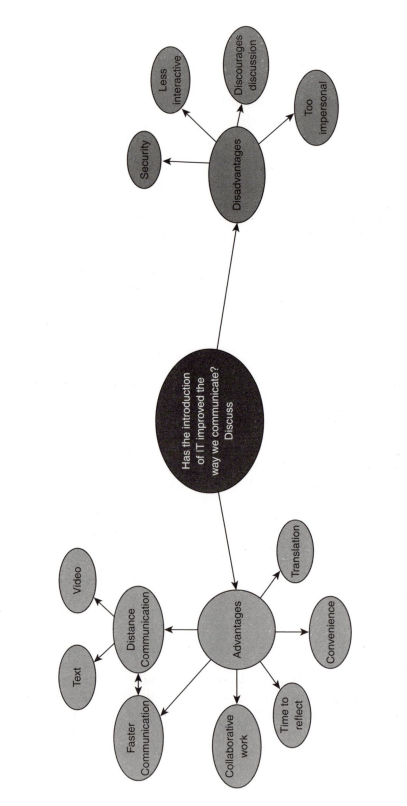

Figure 5.2   Mind Map™ of essay on IT

Plan of the essay based on the concept map for the following question:

Has the introduction of IT improved the way we communicate? Discuss.

I Advantages

A Faster Communication
Delivery time can be measured in seconds.

B Distance Communication
IT has allowed the development of distance learning and enabled students to see their lecturers and other students through chat rooms and Skype.

1 Text
Text can be used in emergencies to alert people to danger.

2 Video (Web Cam)
People can communicate both personally and professionally across the world with the use of Skype and video conferencing.

C Time to reflect
When a request is made by email or text the recipient has a chance to reflect before responding. This is not possible with phone communication. People are not 'put on the spot'.

D Convenience
Mobile devices allow people to meet up without difficulty. Any delays or problems can be immediately reported.

E Translation
Potential for direct translation into other languages.

F Collaborative work
Ability to share written work online.

II Disadvantages

A Too impersonal
Directives can be given and policy set without recourse to discussion. Loses the benefit of non-verbal communication: facial expression and body language.

B Discourages discussion
Subordinates concerned that comments can be kept and used against them. Also emails can be changed whereas hard copy can't be changed.

C Less interactive
Lacks the benefit of group discussion and developmental consensus.

D Security
Prone to hacking.

At this stage of your plan **you may decide to reconsider the order** in which you intend to present your argument and you should **change the order if it would be more appropriate**. This is simply done by cutting and pasting.

If the intention was to write the essay in the order of the arguments presented above, you might expand either theme into an introduction something like the one below:

Possible Introduction based on Theme 2 above:

There are many advantages in the way we communicate since the introduction of IT such as faster communication over long distances through both text and video. It also allows people time to reflect before responding and time can be set for collaborative communication which simulates face-to-face discussions. There is also the facility of instant translation of text when working in different cultures and languages and the convenience of these innovations cannot be overstated. Conversely some of these advantages can create problems such as directives being sent out without recourse to discussion and employees sometimes feel that email can be used against them as it can be changed. This can be especially true in a large organisation in different cities or countries where staff cannot communicate with each other. IT is also prone to hacking. However, there is no doubt that the advantages of IT far outweigh the disadvantages in our daily communication and probably the greatest advantage is the speed of that communication.

This is the time in your essay planning and writing where **you need to research the areas in which you need information**. It is also the point at which you must consider how much time you have available and allocate time to the various areas.

Writing the essay in workable 'chunks'

This allows you to see your progress and know that you are achieving your goals, staying on task and not feeling stressed. An example of this is to **look at the word count and to break it up into paragraphs** as the outline above shows and to allocate the number of words across the essay to fit in with the number of paragraphs. It obviously doesn't have to be precise but it will help you stay on task and not spend too much time on one area to the detriment of others. **Don't forget that all essays need an introduction, which takes about 10% to 12% of the word count, and a conclusion, which takes between 10% to 12% of the word count.**

Examples of chunking your essay depending on the word count

Table 5.2 gives some examples of how you might be able to break up essays of different lengths into manageable chunks and distribute the word count across your plan. Some paragraphs will obviously be longer than others, but if you have an overall idea of about how many words you should allocate to each section of your essay you will see that it is not such a formidable task and it will also prevent you from spending too much time on one aspect of the essay at the expense of other sections.

Table 5.2   Word lengths of sections in typical essays

Total length of essay	2,000 words	5,000 words	10,000 words
Introduction	200 words	500 words	1,000 words
Body paragraphs	4 paragraphs of 400 words	8 paragraphs of 500 words	16 paragraphs of 500 words
	or	or	or
	5 paragraphs of 300 words	9 paragraphs of 450 words	17 paragraphs of 450 words
Conclusion	200–250 words	500–600 words	1,000–1,200 words

Some common forms of essay planning include **SWOT (Strengths, Weaknesses, Opportunities and Threats)** Analyses and a template for these has been prepared on the CD-ROM to help you.

(GO to SWOT Template and Example on CD-ROM)

Another useful form of essay planning especially in the Social Sciences is related to thinking of issues in respect to major factors such as **PEST (Political, Economic, Social and Technological)** issues. A template for this is also included on the CD-ROM. It is also known as **STEP (Social, Technological, Economic and Political)**.

(GO to PEST Analysis Template and Example on CD-ROM)

Referencing, plagiarism and the use of sources

Most assignments will require you to draw upon the writings, research and ideas of others. Every time you state a fact or make an assertion in your piece you should support it with a reference to an original source. **Plagiarism is the use of another person's ideas or findings as your**

own by simply copying them and reproducing them without due acknowledgement. Plagiarism is dishonest and constitutes cheating. If discovered (and it will be), it is severely dealt with and may result in your exclusion from a course. Plagiarism is easily detected by university staff from changes in style, tone and vocabulary in the submitted work. Moreover institutions are increasingly using electronic tools, such as Turnitin to compare submitted work against electronic databases of text (http://www.submit.ac.uk/static_jisc/ac_uk_index.html).

Different organisations, universities, colleges, journals and professional groups have their own preferred methods of referencing. Requirements for referencing in assignments vary between institutions and need to be strictly observed. Ask your tutor for the referencing guidelines for your course.

Referencing

There are basically two major methods of referencing:

- Footnote/Endnote system
- Harvard system.

Footnote/Endnote system
This a numeric reference in the footer at the bottom of the page or end of the essay.

An example:

> ... 'Even after practice, people cannot accurately understand rapid discourse above a definite rate. This maximum rate is 300 words per minute – again ten syllables per second'.[1]

(Foot of page or end of section, chapter or essay):

1. D. Orr, H. Friedman and J. Williams, 'Trainability of listening comprehension of speeded discourse', *Journal of Educational Psychology* 56 (1965), pp. 148–56.

Harvard system
This system uses a brief citation in the text in brackets, with a full reference in the bibliography at the end of the document.

> ... 'Even after practice, people cannot accurately understand rapid discourse above a definite rate. This maximum rate is 300 words per minute – again ten syllables per second' (Orr, Friedman and Williams, 1965, pp. 148–56).

Microsoft Word provides facilities to help you insert citations and the bibliography into your essay.

) (GO to Inserting Citations and References in MS Word Documents on CD-ROM)

Bibliography

The bibliography comes at the end of the whole piece. All books, articles and other sources referred to in the text should be listed on a reference page(s) at the end of the paper. Entries are arranged alphabetically by author surname.

With footnotes or endnotes – simply restate the details already given in the note, but with the authors' surnames first:

Orr, D., Friedman, H. and Williams, J., 'Trainability of listening comprehension of speeded discourse', *Journal of Educational Psychology* 56 (1965), pp. 148–56.

With Harvard system – give all publication details, as shown in the footnote above, but with authors' surnames first. Often the date of publication is placed immediately after the surnames as with their referencing system.

Orr, D., Friedman, H. and Williams, J. (1965) 'Trainability of listening comprehension of speeded discourse', *Journal of Educational Psychology* 56, pp. 148–56.

This is a very brief explanation of the two systems of referencing; it is vital to look up your university or college course guide. There is a link to a typical referencing guide on the CD-ROM:

) (GO to Bournemouth University Acadamic Support Library Citing References on CD-ROM)

Finishing up

Finally always remember to reread and edit your work at least 24 hours after you have finished your essay, so that what you are reading is what you have written and not what you think you have written. Some students find using a text reader, such as Read&Write, ClaroRead or SpeakQ very useful at the editing stage as some dyslexic students cannot see their errors but they can hear them.

Getting your essay back from your tutor

When you get your essay back from your tutor you should read their comments carefully, and in a positive frame of mind. They are intended to be supportive and the advice they give can be used in the future to help with your next essay. So if you don't understand them, do not hesitate to ask your tutor to explain them.

Some comments will be on the content of the essay, and others will be directed towards structure and language. Insufficient or incorrect content indicates that you may need to do more research and widen your reading. Comments suggesting that you have not answered the questions mean that you need to spend more time analysing the question and planning your work. If you feel that the comments on language and structure are beyond your capabilities to correct, you should seek help from the college learning support or dyslexia support teams.

Planning checklist

The checklist shown in Table 5.3 has been made out for the first essay question discussed in the chapter. This template is available on the CD-ROM.

(GO to Planning Your Essay – Checklist on CD-ROM)

 **points to remember**

In preparing and planning your essays:

- analyse the question and work out what it is asking you to do
- work out the type of essay the question requires
- underline the key words
- think about the general issues relating to the question and prepare a Mind Map™
- write a theme for your essay to give it direction
- organise your concept map into a sequence of points or essay plan
- reorganise this plan in the light of your research to make sure it flows well
- write your essay in workable chunks of text so that you can see what you are achieving and don't lose the direction of your argument
- be prepared to seek or ask for more expert help if this is appropriate
- check your references
- reread and edit your work.

Table 5.3   Planning your essay – checklist

Unpacking the question	Instruction words: **Discuss**				
	Key words: **'Global warming** is the **greatest threat** we face.'				
Essay type	Expository	Explanatory	Interpretive	Evaluative	Argumentative
				X	

Brainstorm	What you know
	Issues
	• Rich countries way ahead industrially • Must realise that poorer countries need to industrialise • CO_2 • Changing weather patterns

	• Flooding
	   • Droughts
	   • Melting of polar ice
	   • Rising sea levels

	• Ways forward

	• Reducing use of fossil fuels
	   • Stopping deforestation
	   • Increasing rainforest
	   • Protecting and increasing native forests as 'carbon storehouses'
	   • Concensus

	What you need to research
	• Amount of CO_2 produced in both the industrialised and newly industrialised countries • Changing weather patterns • Examples of flooding and drought followed by famine • Amounts of polar ice melting • Sea level rises • Amount of rainforest destroyed every year • Amount of new forests planted and cultivated • Conferences in Toyko and Copenhagen

Theme	**Direction**: Essay is actually asking you to examine the statement that 'global warming is the greatest threat we face'.
	Global warming is the greatest threat we face as unless countries come to some agreement about the amount of CO_2 which is being put into the atmosphere we will face continual climate change which involves devasting floods and droughts which cause famine. The melting of polar ice and the rise of sea levels have the potential to wipe out whole civilisations.

Chunks	Introduction: expanding the theme Body paragraphs:
	• Comparison of the industrialised and newly industrialised countries • Emissions of CO_2 around the world • Changing weather patterns including floods and droughts • Melting of polar ice and changes in sea level • Ways forward such as reduction of use of fossil fuels, stopping deforestation and starting reforestation and regeneration • Outcomes of the conferences in Tokyo and Copenhagen
	Conclusion: summing up your points

CD-ROM Contents

Please go to the CD-ROM accompanying this book to find the following documents:

Essay Planning for Jane Eyre Question	Word Document
Global Warming	Word Document
Has the Introduction of IT Improved the Way we Communicate?	Word Document
Inserting Citations and References in MS Word Documents	Word Document
IT Mind Map™	Word Document
PEST Analysis Example	Word Document
PEST Analysis Template	Word Document
Planning your Essay – Checklist	Word Document
SWOT Example	Word Document
SWOT Template	Word Document

Please go to the CD-ROM accompanying this book to find links to the following:

BibWord Microsoft Word Citation and Bibliography Styles
Bournemouth University Academic Support Library Citing References
Create a Bibliography in MS Word
Free Mind Mapping Software
How to Write Footnotes, Endnotes, Electronic References and Bibliographies in a Proper Format
Inspiration Software
MindManager Software
Zotero Research Tool

6

Structuring Different Writing Genres

Helen Birkmyre

developmental objectives

This chapter:

- describes the difficulties that are faced by dyslexic students when attempting to write in different genres
- provides advice for constructing sentences
- outlines a simple formula for paragraph writing – the Point Evidence Comment (PEC) method – and thus helps you to write coherent paragraphs
- provides a framework for reports
- outlines the function of abstracts, literature reviews and reflections and how to construct them.

Constructing coherent sentences

Essay writing, whether for coursework or examination script, is the predominant method of assessment after the age of 16 but many subjects require different forms of writing. Arguably, college or university students experience more difficulty with formal writing than any other task. This is because it requires so **many different skills** that need to be performed simultaneously, such as generating ideas, getting them down on paper, sentence, construction, spelling and grammar. Dyslexic students often have trouble expressing their ideas clearly and in a logical, sequential order.

The basic unit of all forms of writing is the sentence. The most common problem amongst dyslexic students is the tendency to write long, rambling sentences containing a multiplicity of points or ideas. Basically, a sentence should contain one idea or point. This does not necessarily mean that all sentences are short and simple as ideas can be qualified or modified with related statements. It simply means that if you are introducing another idea or topic that is not related to the main idea you should start a new sentence. If your sentence goes over three lines see if you can split it up. Remember that it easy for a reader to become lost in long, rambling disconnected sentences. Reflect on how difficult you find long sentences to read in academic text and think of your reader. Finally check that each of your sentences has a subject and a verb which agrees in person and number. (See Chapter 8 'The parts of a sentence'.)

Constructing coherent paragraphs

In the same way that a sentence is one idea, a paragraph is a set of related ideas. A common problem for dyslexic students is including lots of points in one paragraph without fully explaining them. Dyslexic students also tend to meander, and repeat themselves, finding it difficult to make points clearly. An effective way to tackle these problems is to create a framework for the information using the Point Evidence Comment (PEC) paragraph formula, which can be found in *The Good History Student's Handbook* (Pleuger, 2000). This formula can be used for writing essays as well as the other writing genres: reports and reflective learning journals.

The *Collins Online Dictionary* defines 'paragraph' as follows:

> [in a piece of writing] one of a series of subsections each usually devoted to one idea and each usually marked by the beginning of a new line, indentation, increased interlinear space, etc.

You can think of your paragraphs as being mini essays, with an introduction (point), main body (evidence) and comment (conclusion) (see Figure 6.1). Gordon Jarvie, in the *Bloomsbury Grammar Guide* (2000), states that 'a paragraph should be seen as a unit of thought and not a unit of length'. You should consider only one point per paragraph. Having one point per paragraph makes it easier for the reader to process the information being provided. You will not be rewarded with a good mark if you do not fully explain the points you are making.

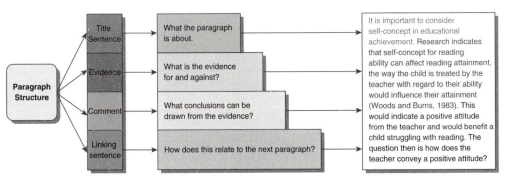

Figure 6.1 Paragraph structure

Point

After you have interpreted the question carefully and decided on the points you wish to include, using a concept map or similar form of brainstorming (see Chapter 5, pp. 57–59), you can begin to structure your essay using the PEC formula. **You should first make sure that the point you are making relates directly to the question asked**. Ask yourself, 'Does this point relate to the question?' If it does, then keep it in your essay. If not, leave it out. Irrelevant points can only weaken your argument. The **first sentence is also known as the topic sentence** because it lets the reader know what the topic of the paragraph is. In the opening paragraph of the introduction this sentence should refer to the question or title.

Evidence

It is vital that you support your point with relevant evidence. **Evidence can be quotations from reliable sources, statistics, examples or visual images**. You can use more than one of these to back up your argument. The stronger the evidence you can provide, the less likely the marker will be to deduct marks. An excellent account of how to use evidence is provided by Bryan Greetham in *How to Write Better Essays* (2001).

Comment

This is your opportunity to demonstrate **your ability to critique and analyse the information you have provided**. In order to demonstrate your point of view it is not sufficient to merely make the point. You have to comment on it as well. **A sentence or two enables you to explain why your point is relevant**. Do not write, 'I think that ...'. Academic conventions dictate that **you do not normally write in the first person** except in reflective journals and similar pieces of work where you will be encouraged to write in the first person. (See the 'Reflective learning journals' section below.) Check with your lecturer, if you are uncertain.

The phrase that you use for your comment will depend on the strength of your evidence, as shown below:

If the evidence is strong:

- It is clear, therefore, that ... .
- It is without doubt the case that ... .
- It is evident that ... .
- Therefore, it is probable that ... .
- It is likely that ... .

If the evidence is less strong:

- It is possible that ... .
- It is unlikely that ... .
- It could be argued that ... .
- The evidence suggests that ... .

---

case study – using PEC

Kate, a student who had just started her first year of university, required assistance with her essay writing because she was not fulfilling her potential. Her grades for these were low average to below average for her A-level work. Structuring her essays, paragraphing and sequencing points were her greatest weaknesses. Her answers tended to wander aimlessly, lacking structure. She was unsure of how to introduce an essay so they were weak from the very beginning. She had points that belonged in the conclusion in the introduction and there was an overall lack of coherence. Some of her paragraphs were very long and were not written correctly. She had many points in her paragraphs that were undeveloped. Some of her paragraphs were not relevant because she had not made it clear how they related to the question. This can happen when a point is not introduced clearly. Kate often didn't support her points with evidence, using few examples to substantiate her claims. She needed to get into the habit of making a point, supporting it with evidence and then commenting on the evidence in order that her essays had a coherent argument and structure. It was clear that Kate had the ability to make good points as there were many in her work but they were not substantiated or explained fully. She had no idea about the function of a paragraph or how to structure one.

As a result of her difficulties her essays had no clear argument and she failed to answer the questions properly. After working on analysing essay questions and paragraph structure, her first university essay was a remarkable improvement on her previous essays. On her lecturer's marking sheet for the essay she was given 'very good' for 'understanding and discussion of relevant material', and a 'very good' for 'identification of key points and coherent essay structure'. The tutor commented that it was 'well-organised material and focused'. The tutor also said it was one of the best in the year. By using strategies to analyse the question and using the PEC formula for paragraphing, Kate's essay writing went from mediocre to one of the best examples in her year.

Linking paragraphs

Even assuming that you are able to have a clear purpose and a good plan, there are techniques used by good writers to get everything to 'hang together'. Each paragraph will be related to the one before and the one after. This is **coherence**.

There are two main techniques that you can use to help in achieving coherence:

- Try to use words that signal to the reader the connection between ideas. Words like **'therefore'**, **'thus'**, **'hence'**, **'on the other hand'**, **'conversely'**, **'secondly'**, **'for example'** and **'similarly'** tie ideas together or to the main theme of your essay. They direct the reader's attention to the relationships that you are proposing.
- By repeating key words again, the reader's attention is drawn back to the main theme and the relationship of this particular paragraph to it. Key words and key ideas are used too seldom in many essays and while their absence can affect the reader (by making the essay hard to follow), their absence can also affect the writer.

   Thus, you may find that because you did not use a key word, that your own attention has wandered off the main theme and that you are including irrelevant material. Thus the repetition of key words is valuable on at least two counts.
- Of course the repetition of the same word again and again may irritate the reader. An alternative method is to use another word or phrase with the same meaning. For instance, instead of using the phrase 'key words' in the above paragraph, I could have used such phrases as **'important words'**, **'central ideas'** or **'key themes'**.
- You may use a thesaurus to help you find words that may be substituted for others. A word of warning, however – it is unwise to change a simple word for a complex one.

If you practise trying to get coherence in your essays, you will certainly succeed. Your writing may win no prizes for literature, but then no one has won a prize for literature whose writing did not cohere.

Writing reports, abstracts, literature reviews and reflective learning journals

Before you begin writing assessed pieces of work **ensure that you have read your handbook and/or criteria for the piece of work**. The handbook should specify the elements that need to be included, such as an abstract, literature review, methodology and/or results section. If it does not, ask your tutor to tell you what is required.

Reports

Report writing is required for numerous subjects and it is important that you write it in the conventional report-writing format, unless instructed otherwise. Once again, you should follow the PEC formula for paragraphing within reports, where required. However, it is likely that you will need to include paragraphs that do not follow the PEC formula and that are made up of sentences describing or defining a subject for the reader, for instance as in the METHOD section in Table 6.1.

Table 6.1   Format for reports

I	INTRODUCTION	(a) outline the aims (including hypothesis of the experiment)
		(b) summarise empirical literature relevant to the hypothesis to be evaluated
		(c) offer methodological criticisms of relevant studies, if they are related to the hypothesis of the experiment
		(d) if it seems necessary, define any key terms, comparing the definitions with operational criteria used in the experiment
II	METHOD	Describe:
		(a) the subjects of the experiment
		(b) the materials and/or apparatus
		(c) the procedure, including all details which someone who wanted to repeat the experiment would need to know
III	RESULTS	(a) present data yielded by the experiment in summary form (the raw data is usually included in an Appendix)
		(b) offer just a brief description of the data, but no discussion of its theoretical significance
IV	DISCUSSION	(a) connect results with explicit aims of experiment (refer to introduction)
		(b) review results in relation to general theory
V	CONCLUSION	This is sometimes separated out from the DISCUSSION, or may be included within it. It should make clear what new facts can be stated as a result of the experiment.

(GO to Report Writing Template on CD-ROM)

Deal with the piece of work chunk by chunk. If you find yourself getting 'stuck' on one area, leave it for some time and move on to another section. It is likely that when you come back to the section you were 'stuck' on you will have thought of a new perspective to bring to it.

Abstracts

An abstract is an overview of your piece of work. It is not an introduction. Your introduction is a separate entity. It is best to leave writing the abstract until after you have completed the piece, unless it is required as an indication of a paper or presentation which is to follow. They are traditionally required for conference programmes so that delegates can choose the sessions they wish to attend. **They need to be an accurate reflection of what the paper, presentation or report will include.**

Abstracts are required for some pieces of work but not others. It is likely that your lecturer will tell you whether or not you will be required to write one or it will be stated in the criteria for the piece of work.

The Online Writing Lab (OWL) of Purdue University provides excellent instructions for writing abstracts for reports. The author argues that there are **two types of abstract: informational and descriptive**. Both informational and descriptive abstracts should give an overview of the contents of the report. See: http://owl.english.purdue.edu/

- **Informational** abstracts should include information about each section of your report: purpose, methods, scope, results, conclusions and recommendations. They should be up to 10% of the report in length.
- **Descriptive** abstracts discuss the purpose, method and scope of the report but **not** the results, conclusions and recommendations. They should be around 100 words.

The Online Writing Lab highlights that an abstract should be made up of one or more paragraphs that are **succinct and focused**. You should give the overview of the contents of the report **in the order in which you placed them** in your text. **It should not provide any information that is not included in the report itself**. It should also be written in such a way that people who are not specialists in the field you are researching can understand what your project is about.

The Online Writing Lab also suggests four steps for writing report abstracts.

- Reread your report to **pick out the key points** to include in your abstract. Highlight them as you read through it. Pick the key points from each of these sections: purpose, methods, scope, results, conclusions and recommendations.

73

- Write a first draft of your abstract without looking at your report with the purpose, methods, scope, results, conclusions and recommendations in your mind. Do not lift sentences from your report.
- Revise your first draft to deal with any **structural and sequencing problems such as placing of sentences**. **Edit out any information that is irrelevant**. Add any information that is relevant or that is missing. Make sure that your sentences are succinct. Correct any errors in grammar or spelling.
- Proofread your final draft.

If you follow these steps, you should be able to compose a clear and concise abstract.

Literature reviews

For dissertations, case studies, projects and essays you may be required to write a review of the literature on the topic that is the focus of your research. For those reading history this is called the historiography, which is a discussion of the historical literature written on a subject. **The literature review should follow your introduction and is placed before the main body of the essay**.

Writing a literature review is a useful exercise and will help you to gain a broader knowledge of the subject and help develop your ability to analyse and develop critical thinking.

In your literature review you should:

- **Demonstrate your understanding** of the existing knowledge and theories on that subject.
- **Highlight** any debate or controversial issues that are significant.
- **Critique the literature** highlighting the strengths and weaknesses of it and any theories that have been proposed that are more plausible.
- **Establish your opinion** in relation to the authors' views and comment on them. You must not merely describe what the authors have said. In order to get a good mark it is necessary for you to provide your own opinion on the matter, for instance agreeing with one point of view or another, or elements of the different arguments.

The University of Toronto's Writing at the University of Toronto site has an excellent page on Literature Reviews, providing a list of questions to ask yourself about your literature to ensure that you include all the elements that you need. See: http://www.writing.utoronto.ca/home

When writing your literature review use the PEC strategy in order that you can make your point, support it with evidence and comment on it.

Reflective learning journals

Some courses will require that you keep a set of reflections on what you have learnt throughout your course and your opinions on it. This type of writing is more informal than academic writing and you have more freedom of expression. Phyllis Creme (2000) calls this type of writing, "'the personal", in University writing'. There are no strict rules that you need to follow; however, here are some guidelines. You should:

- Write in the **first person** – using 'I'.
- Consider **relevant points** that were mentioned in your class and in your research and **your opinion on them** – establishing a critical position.
- Make points about **significant academic texts** and what they mean to you.
- Discuss what you have **learnt**.
- Discuss what you have felt **inspired by**.
- Highlight what **you do not understand fully** and how you plan to go about finding out **more information** on the topic.
- Discuss your **successes and failures**. If you have been successful, try to evaluate why you were. If you failed to do something well, try to evaluate what went wrong and why, and how you can improve.

Keeping your reflective learning journal and expressing your thoughts in a personal manner should help you to:

- process the information relating to your course;
- increase your understanding of the topic;
- establish a **critical position** on the topics you are studying.

Write in logical paragraphs using the PEC formula for many of the paragraphs. You will still be required to provide evidence to support the points you are making and comment on that evidence for much of your writing, despite it being a more personal style.

Writing for the new media

It may be that you are required to contribute to a blog or a wiki as part of your course. Although this could be an individual task, it is more likely to be part of a collaborative project (see Chapter 11 – 'Collaborative Learning'). Tim Berners-Lee, the World Wide Web pioneer thought of the web as an interactive, communication space where ' ... everybody would be putting their ideas in, as well as taking them out' (1999).

To share knowledge on the internet, or university intranet, requires the same principles of **clarity** and **organisation** as other forms of writing. As with reflections there are no fixed rules, but:

- **Keep it short**. Do not write long, dense blocks of text.
- If you want to express an opinion, do so, but be **polite**.

- Use lots of links to other sources of information.
- Use formatting, colour, pictures and diagrams to make your contribution visually interesting.
- Use lists.
- Be informal, but do not use slang, nor 'textese'.
- Check your spelling.

points to remember

- Use the simple formula for paragraph writing – the Point Evidence Comment (PEC) method.
- Write reports under the headings suggested.
- Make sure that your abstracts cover the contents of your presentation, paper or report and that they are concise and clear.
- Read widely and write clear literature reviews to increase your knowledge and establish your line of argument.
- Write reflective learning journals in the first person and more informal prose to help you understand the subject you are studying.

CD-ROM Contents

Please go to the CD-ROM accompanying this book to find the following documents:

Report Writing Template   Word Document

Please go to the CD-ROM accompanying this book to find links to the following:

Garbl's Writing Centre
Guardian Style Guide
How to Write for the Web
Monash University Academic Writing Skills
OWL at Purdue
Wiki Writing
Writing Effective Reflections

7

The Dissertation

Cheri Shone

developmental objectives

This chapter explains:

- the importance of critical thinking
- dissertation format
- exploring your resources
- planning
- reading
- writing
- presentation.

What is a dissertation?

The culmination of most degrees in the United Kingdom would include a dissertation. The form of dissertations varies across different subjects but essentially all are pieces of independent work in which students are required to 'collect, organise and analyse information on a title of their choice and come to conclusions based on solid argument' (Walliman, 2005, p. 3). The process of writing can be difficult for any student and an extended piece of writing that involves a lot of reading and takes a lot of planning can cause panic for a dyslexic student. The good news is that the **strengths associated with a**

dyslexic profile listed below are those that can make your work innovative and exciting.

- Approaching academic issues from unusual perspectives.
- Making unusual connections.
- Being creative in producing new ideas easily.
- Being good at 'what if' *problematics.*
- Being good at following a passionate interest. (Cooper in Pollok, 2009, p. 66.)

This chapter and others in this book will help you deal with those aspects of the process of dissertation writing that you find more problematic.

Choosing your topic

This is often the hardest thing for many students. As it is going to require a lot of your time and effort it is important that you are fully engaged with it and so choose something you care about and to which you are very committed. Other things to consider about the topic are:

- Is it manageable in terms of size with consideration to both time and resources? (Don't choose something which is too big to handle.)
- Is there sufficient material available for a literature review?
- Is it unique but within a recognisable context?
- Will it help your future development and career?
- Is it acceptable to your supervisor?
- If it is not a subject on which your supervisor is knowledgeable or interested, you will be on your own; are you prepared for this?

What skills are you expected to demonstrate through writing your dissertation?

The importance of critical thinking

You will be expected to construct a critical argument that demonstrates your ability to **analyse, synthesise and evaluate** the reading you are doing around your chosen title.

Firstly **analyse** the reading you are doing. You need to ask:

- What do you think about what you are reading?
- What points are the authors trying to make?
- How do these ideas relate to each other?

78

- How do these ideas differ from each other?
- What biases do you and the authors have?
- What assumptions are you and the authors making?

Secondly **synthesise** what you have read to **make connections between the viewpoints**. The advantage that a dyslexic student has is the ability to see the bigger picture and make unusual connections. This plus has to be tempered with the tendency to lose track of the argument that is being pursued and to follow new trains of thought not directly related to the question at hand. One way of avoiding this pitfall is to put the title of the dissertation up on your wall or in the header of your draft document so that you can check that the work you are doing is relevant to the topic you have chosen.

Thirdly **evaluate** the evidence that you have assembled:

- Do the various authors agree or disagree?
- How valid are their arguments and what are their reputations in their chosen fields?
- How and why have you used the evidence to draw your own conclusions and to support your arguments?

Dissertation format

The next thing that you need to consider is the format of the dissertation. **Each discipline will have its own requirements**; an arts dissertation may require images and innovation whereas scientific report writing has a required format that is prescribed. It is important that you are well versed in these requirements.

One way of keeping this format clear in your mind and ensuring that you develop the argument within the word count parameter is to create a template of the structure of your dissertation. This will allow you to get a clear idea of the word count, the development and structure of your argument.

(GO to Dissertation Templates on CD-ROM)

Thus far we have considered a written dissertation but in some universities it is also possible to ask to be allowed to present your work in an alternative format if you feel that your dyslexia would prove a serious barrier to a piece of written work (see Symonds, 2008). One of the options available is a **Viva Voce** which is essentially **an oral presentation of your work**. It would be a mistake to think that this would be a 'soft' option. The presentation would still have to fulfil all the academic criteria of a written dissertation and it could be argued that it would require more work than a written dissertation because it is not yet that common a format and as such would need more input from both the student and department. If this is an option you want to consider, it would be advisable to start talking to your department well in advance to explore if this would be a viable option for you.

Exploring your resources

As with any other task you face in the course of your study the more effectively you utilise your resources the better the quality of the work you are going to produce. There are many resources available to you; one of the most important relationships is with **your supervisor**. Think about who will be supervising your dissertation and whether their teaching and communication style suits yours. It is important that you have a good idea of what you both expect from each other.

- How often will you be meeting up?
- What level of support can you expect?
- What is the best way to keep in touch with each other?

If you have a Dictaphone or mobile phone that can make recordings it is a good idea to **record the sessions** so that you have a record of what was said.

---

case study

Lucy had chosen her dissertation topic with little thought to her dissertation supervisor. She had worked with him in the past and sometimes found his instructions difficult to follow but had not thought about how this would impact on her in relation to her dissertation. The supervisor was often in a rush which made it difficult for Lucy to make clear notes on the sessions they had together. This made Lucy feel anxious. Lucy needs clear guidelines to structure her work and found that some of the guidance she received from her dissertation supervisor unclear. She said that in retrospect she feels that she would have given more thought to who was going to supervise her dissertation and how that relationship would impact on her work.

Think about areas of the dissertation you would find problematic and then see who would be in the best position to help you. For example, your supervisor may be in the best position to help you with questions about the topic of your dissertation and your dyslexia tutor could be the person to ask about planning.

If you are anxious about writing, your **university may offer courses on dissertation writing** or have a writing course you could attend. **It is worthwhile looking at dissertations from previous years to get an idea of format and writing styles**.

Resources also mean the books, journals, websites and any other material you use. It is worth **approaching the staff of the library to see if they can offer you help with accessing books, journals and online resources** in the university. Make sure the resources you use are credible. It is never acceptable to use sites such as Wikipedia in an academic context.

Be creative about your use of Assistive and Information Technology (AT and IT). For example create a Mind Map™ or word document with all the email addresses you need, such as the library, your supervisor, journal links, people you want to contact for research.

Planning

A dyslexic student may have problems with 'sensing the passage of time, sequencing over time and planning time' (Cooper in Pollok, 2009, pp. 66–7) all of which are essential to work effectively on a dissertation. Students often think that study is unremitting hard work and any activity that doesn't have you sweating blood can seem like displacement activity. Planning and organisation of your workload can often be fun. **Identify what you need to do** and decide which activities will require a lot of concentration (reading and writing) and those activities that are less onerous (making a list of journals you want to source, making graphs of your results, updating your bibliography). You will then be able to **intersperse the easier tasks with those that are more difficult** in order to work more effectively. Pushing the time you spend at the desk does not necessarily increase the amount of work you complete. The written work you produce when you are tired often takes longer to write and is less coherent. Plan your work with your work pace in mind rather than that suggested by the dissertation schedule. It is possible to ask for an **accommodated submission** dependent on your assessment report and your university's policies, but bear in mind that if you do have an extension for your hand-in dates it may interfere with other work that you have to do.

Plan for bad days and feelings of panic. They happen to everyone and they can get in the way of the best work schedule. If you are panicking or having a bad day, give yourself a break, call a friend, have a bath, go for a walk. **Plan breaks and rewards into your schedule**.

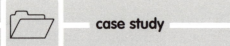

case study

May was a textile student who was assessed as dyslexic in the final year of her degree.

I found that planning helped me to manage my dissertation. I learned how to develop a timetable that suited me and this improved my time keeping. Having a timetable listing important dates and hand-ins for the months leading up to the final submission was essential. I also developed a weekly time planner, listing more specific tasks for that week; this made each stage of the dissertation feel much more manageable and less overwhelming. Once you have mastered a structure that works for your day-to-day life, you begin to appreciate that factoring in breaks and not dedicating the whole day to one specific task, but breaking it up with different tasks can actually help you to achieve more, because you are more focused.

Understanding the Module Handbook

The briefs and instructions for a dissertation can often be a text dense document with important information often not clearly identified; instructions such as word counts, formats and submission dates can easily be overlooked by the dyslexic reader. You can **identify the key information using a highlighter**. The practical information on submission dates and room numbers can be included on a timetable. It is important to include all significant dates and the commitments you have over this period; this will give you an idea of the timeline. Other information such as the structure and layout of the dissertation can be conceptualised using a Mind Map™ or Word document.

Figure 7.1 is an example of part of a plan for a dissertation proposal identifying some of the key points taken from the dissertation brief.

(GO to the CD-ROM for a colour example of a Dissertation Structure)

The following are some of the things you may need to consider:

- binding
- font
- line spacing
- cover page
- abstract (for some dissertations)
- contents page
- page numbers
- number of copies

- headings
- images, tables, statistical results
- appendix
- formatting of references and bibliography.

Some dissertations, for example a PhD, include a viva. Viva dissertation supervisors often require either a poster or PowerPoint presentation of your dissertation topic. Make sure you know well ahead of time what sort of resources you will need and where to find them. It is a good idea to practise your presentation so that you can make sure you are within the time limit.

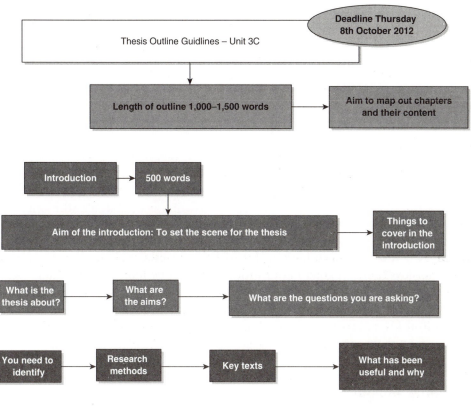

Figure 7.1 Dissertation structure

Reading

A dissertation requires an enormous amount of reading which can make it difficult to manage. The ability of a dyslexic student to make unusual connections can make it difficult to stay focused on the narrow remit of the dissertation topic. A disciplined approach to reading, however, will help you stay on track. There are **two stages to reading**:

- **Background reading to identify and firm up topic areas**. At this stage it is a good idea to Mind Map™ the ideas and concepts that you are reading so that you get an overview of your topic area.
- The second stage is **more focused reading once the key research questions of your dissertation are defined**. At this stage it is a good idea to keep a copy of the dissertation title in a prominent place so that you can constantly refer to it to confirm that the reading you are doing is relevant.

It is important to organise your reading in a way that makes it easy to find the information you need when you come to write. There are a number of ways you can do this:

- You can identify the various topic areas you are going to address with either colour or images (e.g. everything to do with a particular theory identified with a red tag or a blue highlighter).
- Keep a running reference list using either the Word referencing or tools such as Endnote or Zotero.
- Use voice-to-text software such as Dragon or Macspeak to keep a record of quotations you want to use, identifying page numbers, publications and book titles.
- Make sure any photocopies you make have all the relevant information for your referencing.

As it is likely that you will be grappling with **unfamiliar terms and new words it is useful to keep a list of these and explanations of what they mean**. It is also useful to have a **list of link words** such as therefore, however, moreover, etc. A good list of link words can be found at the Eden Skills website (http://edenskills.co.uk). It is also useful to have access to a **thesaurus** which gives you groups of words with similar meanings which will help you to find alternative words so that you do not end up repeating the same words and phrases.

Literature review

Most dissertations require a literary review. Some, for example, in history, theology and English literature consist entirely of a literature review. This is a review of the reading related to your dissertation topic and is an ideal opportunity to demonstrate your ability to analyse, synthesise and evaluate the material you have read. This is the section of the dissertation where you show the marker the reading you have done, why you have chosen the reading and how this reading underpins your dissertation. You are essentially giving the reader a flavour of the literature related to the topic under investigation, identifying:

- what is known about the subject
- what is not yet known
- how this relates to your topic
- any controversy in the literature.

You are not listing the material related to the topic but presenting a critical analysis, synthesis and evaluation of the writing in the area, identifying themes and trends in the literature and how they are related to your area of investigation. You need to ask yourself:

- Have you read widely enough from a variety of sources?
- Are the sources you have used reputable?
- Is the material you have used relevant to the topic you have chosen?
- Have you included views opposed to your own?

The key is to be critical about the reading you are doing so ask yourself questions about the author's perspective. What is the point they are trying to make, how well are they making it, what are their biases and how does it relate to other work in the field. See: http://www.essaycoursework.com/howtowriteadissertation/dissertation-literaturereview.php

Writing

You will have a rough idea of your dissertation in the form of notes, Mind Maps™, research papers, books and online material. You now have to arrange your research into a coherent linear structure that demonstrates your ability to analyse, synthesise and evaluate your chosen topic. Cooper says that there is 'an obvious differential between conceptualising and understanding an argument on the one hand, and written expression, organisational structure and writing on the other' (in Pollok, 2009, p. 68). Dyslexic students often have a problem with the linear structure of an academic argument. One way of dealing with this is to **conceptualise the structure of your dissertation graphically breaking it up into its constituent parts**. For example, Figure 7.2 shows the basic structure for a 10,000-word dissertation on Sustainable Food Production.

Introduction	1,000 words What you are going to say	Could be written last
Three main topic areas You can colour code your reading to correspond to the topic areas	Chapter 1: 2,000 words Sustainable Food Production	9 paragraphs of 250 words
	Chapter 2: 2,500 words Current Food Production Practices	8 paragraphs of 250 words
	Chapter 3: 2,500 words The Way Forward (New Practices)	9 paragraphs of 250 words
Conclusion	2,000 words Drawing a conclusion from your evidence	

Figure 7.2   Basic dissertation structure

(GO to the CD-ROM for an example of a Dissertation Structure for a Scientific Report)

Although this may not be exactly how you will distribute your word count in the final draft it will give you an overview of the structure of your dissertation and help you keep track of your argument. If you then break your word count for each chapter up into paragraphs it will give you some idea of the word count you have, to develop each particular part of the argument.

Breaking the task down like this can make it seem less daunting. An added benefit is that by making the structure of your dissertation clear and explicit

Abstract Word count	A synopsis of the research and findings (Could be written last)
Introduction Word count	An introduction of what you are going to cover (Could be written last)
Research Methods Word count	Identify what you need to include Method Participants Data
Results Discussion Word count	Identify the main arguments and colour code them to identify the themes in your reading
Conclusion	Draw a conclusion from your findings relating them to the research in the area Explain why your research did or did not support research in the field

Figure 7.3   Scientific report, 10,000 words

it enables you to concentrate on one element at a time and can help to keep you focused on the information that will help you develop your argument. It also means you don't have to start writing on a blank page. You can embed a copy of this structure in the draft document or put it up on your wall to keep you on track.

If you have not started your reference list while you were reading it is a good idea to start it when you start writing. **Make sure you know the preferred referencing format of your academic department**. If you are not going to use one of the referencing tools mentioned in the reading section then start to create your referencing list as the citations appear in your text. You can either colour code the references or number them to make sure all of your citations appear in the references. If you are typing in the reference list put an example of the format at the top of your bibliography. A good rule is to **make any text that should not appear in the final text a different colour** so that you don't forget to delete it.

It is good practice to **proofread** any piece of written work you do. There are a number of ways you can do this. You can print a hard copy and read it through; you can use software such as ClaroRead or Text Help Gold to read it back to you as it is often easier to hear than see the mistakes. You could also ask someone you trust such as a family member or friend to proofread it for you. There are also proofreading services, although these can prove costly. If you have used speech-to-text software it will read back to you what you have written.

Make sure your work is backed up!

Presentation

If your dissertation looks professional it will make a good impression!

You can now use the checklist you made when you were decoding your dissertation brief to check that you have fulfilled all the requirements of the dissertation brief. Decide if you are going to print your dissertation yourself, use the university printers or have it professionally printed and bound. If you're going to print it yourself:

- Make sure you have enough paper.
- Make sure you have enough ink.
- Make sure you have everything you need to bind your dissertation.
- Make sure you are clear about the format required.

It is good practice to include some sort of identification such as your student number in a header or footer.

If you are using the university printers or a printing service remember:

- Other people will be using these as well so they may be busy.
- Make sure your USB stick or CD works with the computers that will be used when printing.

Remember that the skills you develop on your degree will enable you to work effectively once you are qualified in your chosen field.

- Get as much help as you can from your dissertation supervisor and the other resources provided by your institution.
- Make a plan and stick to it.
- Use a reading strategy and note references as you read.
- Read widely and write clear literature reviews to increase your knowledge and establish your line of argument.
- Good presentation is worth marks.

CD-ROM Contents

Please go to the CD-ROM accompanying this book to find the following documents:

Basic Dissertation Structure	Word Document
Dissertation Plan	Word Document
Scientific Dissertation Structure	Word Document
Writing Your Dissertation	Word Document

Please go to the CD-ROM accompanying this book to find links to the following:

Dissertation Literature Review
Education, Dyslexia and Electronic Needs
Southampton University – Writing Your Dissertation.

8

Improving Your Grammar, Spelling and Punctuation

Sandra Hargreaves and John Brennan

developmental objectives

This chapter outlines the main things you need to know about:

- grammar
- spelling
- punctuation.

Grammar is a topic which many people find difficult, not just dyslexic students. Some basic grammar is essential for writing. This chapter will only deal with the **most essential things** you need. If you would like to know more about grammar, there is more information provided on the CD-ROM. The most important aspects of grammar are:

- the parts of a sentence
- agreement of verb and subject
- the eight parts of speech
- the use of tense.

Spelling can be a difficulty for dyslexic students. This chapter outlines some of the strategies for learning how to spell.

Punctuation is necessary in order to make completely clear what you are trying to say. Incorrect or absent punctuation leads to misunderstanding. The **most important punctuation marks** are:

- full stops
- commas
- apostrophes
- semicolons
- colons
- question marks, and
- exclamation marks.

Grammar

This concerns the systematic understanding of the features of a language. It is not the purpose of this chapter to look at grammar in detail, but you do need some rudimentary knowledge to overcome problems such as why your sentences might not make sense or are ambiguous and rambling.

The parts of a sentence

Sentences normally contain a **subject** and a **verb**. When editing your work, check that your sentences are complete. If the sentence you are editing does not contain a subject and verb, rewrite the sentence so that it does. **Subjects** are **nouns** or **pronouns**. **Verbs** are **action words** or the verb 'to be' and the verb 'to have'. There must also be agreement **between the subject and the verb** so that **singular subjects** must have **singular verbs** and **plural subjects, plural verbs**. If pronouns are involved in the sentence, they also must agree.

> For example: **The boy meets his** friend every morning at the station. (Singular subject, singular verb and singular pronoun)
>
> **The boys meet their** friends every morning at the station. (Plural subject, plural verb and plural pronoun)

Sentences can contain many more elements, and are often very complex but they are not sentences if they do not contain the basic element, that is a **subject and verb agreeing with the subject**, which is known as a finite verb. This unit of subject and finite verb is sometimes called the **sentence kernel**.

The eight parts of speech

All words in a language can be identified as different parts of speech (Table 8.1). Words fall into two broad categories: they can either be **content**

Table 8.1   The eight parts of speech

The eight parts of speech	Content words	1	Nouns
		2	Verbs
		3	Adjectives
		4	Adverbs
	Structure words	5	Pronouns
		6	Prepositions
		7	Conjunctions
		8	Exclamations

words, which have meaning in their own right, such as **nouns, verbs, adjectives** and **adverbs**, or they can be **structure words**, which rely for their meaning on the context of the sentence in which they are used. **Pronouns, prepositions, conjunctions** and **exclamations** fall into the category of structure words.

Finally, on their own, are the articles – definite (the) and indefinite (a or an).

The content words of English

Nouns

A **noun** is the **name** of **something**. There are four types of noun – namely, **common**, **proper**, **collective** and **abstract**. Table 8.2 defines these and gives examples of each.

Table 8.2   Types of nouns

Type	Definition	Example
Common	A **common noun** is a noun referring to a person, place, or thing in a general sense. Usually, you should write it with a capital letter only when it begins a sentence.	All the **gardens** in the **neighbourhood** were invaded by **beetles** this **summer**.
Proper	You always write a **proper noun** with a capital letter, since the noun represents the name of a specific person, place, or thing. The names of days of the week, months, historical documents, institutions, organisations, religions, their holy texts and their adherents are **proper nouns**.	**London Metropolitan University** is near **Holloway Road Tube Station**. **Abraham** appears in the **Talmud** and in the **Koran**.
Collective	A **collective noun** is a noun naming a group of things, animals, or persons. A **collective noun** always takes a singular verb in a sentence.	The **flock** of geese spends most of its time in the pasture.
Abstract	An **abstract noun** is a noun which names anything, which you can *not* perceive through your five physical senses.	He was a man of **principle**. Buying the fire extinguisher was an **afterthought**.

Verbs

Verbs are **action words** plus the verb 'to be' and the verb 'to have'. Whether the events in the sentence are indicated as taking place in the **present** or happened in the **past** is indicated by the **tense** of the verbs used in a sentence. The most important tenses are the **present** and the **past**. Both these tenses consist of three different forms – namely: the simple, the continuous and the perfect. Figure 8.1 shows these different forms.

Note that the simple form of the tense uses only the verb itself. The **continuous** form of the tense uses the verb 'to be' plus the present participle

Present tense

Simple	When she **walks** in the room.
Continuous	I **am walking** in the rain.
Perfect	We **have walked** before.

	Simple	Continuous		Perfect	
I	walk	am	walking	have	walked
You	walk	are		have	
He She It	walks	is		has	
We	walk	are		have	
You	walk	are		have	
They	walk	are		have	

Past tense

Simple	When she **walked** in the room.
Continuous	I **was singing** in the rain.
Perfect	We **had danced** so long ago.

	Simple	Continuous		Perfect	
I	walked	was	walking	had	walked
You	walked	were		had	
He She It	walked	was		had	
We	walked	were		had	
You	walked	were		had	
They	walked	were		had	

Figure 8.1   Verbs and tenses

(**always ends in 'ing'**) of the verb and the perfect form of the tense uses the verb 'to have' and the past participle (**mostly ends in 'ed'**) of the verb.

Adjectives

An **adjective** qualifies a noun or a pronoun by describing, identifying, or quantifying words. Adjectives can be used in their original form or changed to their comparative and superlative forms if comparing two or more things. The box below outlines these uses.

Original	Adjectives can be used before a noun	I like **Chinese** food.
	or after certain verbs.	The coal mines are **dark** and **dank**.
	We can often use two or more adjectives together.	The back room was filled with **large, yellow Wellington** boots.
Comparative	When we talk about two things, we can compare them. We can see if they are the same or different. Perhaps they are the same in some ways and different in other ways. We can use comparative adjectives to describe the differences.	America is big. But Russia is **bigger**. I want to have a **more powerful** computer. Is French **more difficult** than English?
Superlative	A superlative adjective expresses the extreme or highest degree of a quality. We use a superlative adjective to describe the extreme quality of one thing in a group of things.	Canada, China and Russia are big countries. But Russia is the **biggest**. Mount Everest is the **highest** mountain in the world.

Adverbs

An **adverb** is a word that tells us more about (or modifies) a verb, or an adjective or another adverb.

Adverb	An **adverb** modifies a **verb**. But adverbs can also modify **adjectives** or even other **adverbs**.	The man ran **quickly**. Tara is **really** beautiful. It works **very well**.

Many root words in English exist as the four types of function words by simply adding a prefix or suffix, as the box below shows. Certain endings or suffixes such as '**ness**' or '**th**', indicate that a word is a noun while '**en**' indicates a verb and '**ly**' an adverb.

Noun	Verb	Adjective	Adverb
Sweetness	Sweeten	Sweet	Sweetly
Warmth	Warm	Warm	Warmly
Winner	Win	Winning	Winningly
Boldness	Embolden	Bold	Boldly

The structure words of English

The **structure words** of the language **rely** for their meaning **on the context** in which they are used, and include: pronouns, prepositions, conjunctions and exclamations.

Pronouns
A **pronoun** can replace a **noun** or another **pronoun**. You use pronouns like **he**, **which**, and **you** to make your sentences less cumbersome and less repetitive. The two most important types of pronouns are **personal** and **relative**.

Personal pronouns
A **personal pronoun** refers to a specific person or thing and changes its form as shown below:

Person	Number	Gender	Subject	Object	Possessive
1st	Single	Both	I	Me	My
	Plural		We	Us	Our
2nd	Both	Both	You	You	Your
3rd	Single	Male	He	Him	His
		Female	She	Her	Her
		Neuter	It	It	Its
	Plural	Both	They	Them	Their

94

Some examples:

Subjective	**I** was glad to find the bus pass.
	You are surely the strangest child **I** have ever met.
Objective	After reading the pamphlet, Judy threw **it** into the bin.
	Give the list to **me**.
Possessive	**My** life has greatly improved since I changed my job.
	His present is on the kitchen worktop.

Relative pronouns

You can use a **relative pronoun** to link one phrase or clause to another phrase or clause. A clause is a group of words containing at least a subject and verb, but not necessarily a full sentence. The relative pronouns are:

Gender	Subject (before verb)	Object (after verb or preposition)	Possessive
Male Female	who	whom	whose
Neuter	which/that	which/that	

Examples:

Subjective	That is the girl **who** tore her dress. The incident **which** caused the riot, was caused in the paper.
Objective	You may invite **whom** you like to the party.
Possessive	That is the man **whose** car was stolen.

Prepositions

A **preposition** links nouns, pronouns and phrases to other words in a sentence. A preposition usually indicates relationships of some sort:

Time	**After** lunch
Place	**Between** the sheets
Logical	**Against** all odds

As you can see, a preposition is **always** followed by a noun, but there may be an article or adjective in between.

The most common prepositions are: **about, above, across, after, against, along, among, around, at, before, behind, below, beneath, beside, between, beyond, but, by, despite, down, during, except, for, from, in, inside, into, like, near, of, off, on, onto, out, outside, over, past, since, through, through-out, to, towards, under, underneath, until, up, upon, with, within, without**	The book is **on** the table. The book is **beneath** the table. The book is leaning **against** the table. The book is **beside** the table. She held the book **over** the table. She read the book **during** class.

Conjunctions

You can use a **conjunction to link** words, phrases and clauses.

Co-ordinating	You use a **co-ordinating conjunction** to join individual words, phrases, and independent clauses. The **co-ordinating conjunctions** are: **and, but, or, nor, for, so, yet**.	Lilacs **and** violets are usually purple. Daniel's uncle claimed that he spent most of his youth dancing on rooftops **but** not swallowing goldfish.
Subordinating	A **subordinating conjunction** introduces a dependent clause and indicates the nature of the relationship between the clauses. The most common **subordinating conjunctions** are: **after, although, as, because, before, how, if, once, since, than, that, though, until, when, where, whether, while**.	This movie is particularly interesting to feminist film theorists, **because** the screenplay was written by Mae West. **After** she had learned to drive, Alice felt more independent. **If** the paperwork arrives on time, your cheque will be posted on Tuesday. Gerald had to begin his thesis over again **when** his computer crashed.

Correlative	**Correlative conjunctions** always appear in pairs – you use them to link equivalent sentence elements. The most common correlative conjunctions are: **both, and** **either, or** **neither, nor** **not only, but also** **whether, or**.	**Both** my grandfather **and** my father worked in the steel plant. Bring **either** a green salad **or** a fish pie. Corinne is trying to decide **whether** to go to medical school **or** to go to law school. The explosion destroyed **not only** the school **but also** the neighbouring pub.

Exclamation or interjection

An **exclamation** or **interjection** is a word added to a sentence to convey emotion. It is not grammatically related to any other part of the sentence. One usually follows them with an exclamation mark. Both are uncommon in formal academic prose, except in direct quotations.

- **Ouch**, that hurt!
- **Hey**! Put that down.
- **Oh** no, I forgot that the exam was today!

Articles

Articles are the two words we use in English before nouns to make them specific (the) or general (a or an before a vowel).

Articles a an the	When talking about one thing in particular, use **the**. When talking about one thing in general, use **a** or **an** before **a** vowel.	Think of the sky at night. In the sky there is one moon and millions of stars. So normally we could say: I saw **the** moon last night. I saw **a** star last night. I saw **an** array of shooting stars last night.

Most words in English fit into the above categories. If you want to read more about some other words with more specialised uses, go to the CD-ROM.

97

Spelling

Even if you have learnt many strategies for coping with your spelling, there will still be words which give you trouble. The aim of this section is to outline **some basic spelling strategies** which are helpful to most dyslexic students. The most important thing to remember is that you **can learn to spell words** which are **important to you**, and you should never become discouraged or give up. Remember that spelling is largely visual and that you can only be sure of the spelling of a word by looking at it.

Spelling strategies

Look, Say, Cover, Write, Check

One very helpful spelling strategy, which is multi-sensory and which has been used over many years, is the **Look-Say-Cover-Write-Check** method of learning to spell. It involves visual, auditory and kinaesthetic processing. There is a template for this method on the CD-ROM.

(◉) **(GO to Look-Say-Cover-Write-Check Template on CD-ROM)**

You should select **6–12 words** to learn **each week**. These words should be the words **that you want to be able to spell correctly**. They will probably be taken from your subject area or from new areas of professional practice. The method relies on a **multi-sensory approach** to the learning task and **regular practice**. On a template write the words you wish to learn in the first column. The remaining columns should be used over the following week to practise the words at least every second day (see Table 8.3).

Firstly	You should **look carefully** at the word you are trying to learn. In this first step, you will be actually using some of the other strategies mentioned below. You need to **look at the structure of the word**, to see if there are any **whole words within the word** or any **groups of letters** which you can remember as a unit. Another way of looking at the structure is to break the word into syllables.
Secondly	You should **say the word aloud** to your self, **sounding out any sections** you wish to specially remember.
Thirdly	You should cover the word and then write it in the second column. Do not copy the word but cover it and write it. The aim is to put the words in the long-term memory so that they can be recalled correctly.
Finally	You should check the word against the original word in the first column. If you have made a mistake, cross it out and write it in full above the mistake.

Table 8.3   Words displaying a range of spelling strategies

Original Word	Day 1	Day 2	Day 3	Day 4	Final Check
busin**ess**					
sep**arate**					
nec**essa**ry					
accomm**o**dation					
hap**hazard**					
tele**phone**					
doub**tful**					
cir**cle**					
carpen**ter**					
solicit**or**					
gen**ius**					
ingen**ious**					

Continue with this pattern until all columns are used. Do **NOT** try to learn any more than **12** words at one time. Some students prefer to learn only **4–6** at one time.

The words in Table 8.3 have been chosen to specifically demonstrate some of the strategies you might find useful.

Locating a whole word within a larger word

Many students find that if they can locate **a whole word or two within** a larger word, they can remember the larger word. The first two words in Table 8.3 are good examples of words which can be remembered by this strategy. In the word 'business' there are two smaller words, 'bus' and 'i'. In the word 'separate' there are also two, 'a' and 'rat'. Don't forget to use **bright colours** or **diff**erent colo**ured highlight**ing to identify whole words within words.

Using mnemonics to remember spelling

Mnemonics (a Greek word meaning memory trigger, and also difficult to spell) can also be used on the two words analysed above. One way of remembering **business** is the mnemonic: 'I catch the **bus** to **business** every day'. This method combines both the **whole words in the word** with the **memory trick**. A way of remembering **separate** is the mnemonic: 'there is **a rat** in **separate**'. Whatever method you choose, if it works, you have done yourself the favour of learning two commonly misspelt words. Mnemonics can also be used to learn the next two words in the list, which are again difficult and commonly misspelt words. A mnemonic for **necessary** is: 'it is **necessary** to wear **one collar** and two **socks**'. Another for **accommodation** is that: 'good **accommodation** has **two helpings of custard** and **two helpings of meat**'.

Breaking words into sections

'Haphazard' is a good example of a word that is best remembered by breaking it into sections. Otherwise you could be confused by the 'ph' in the middle of the word, which invariably means that the sound 'f' is indicated as in 'telephone'. The operative word to remember here is **hazard** with the prefix 'hap' meaning chance. If you remember it like this, you will never make a mistake of mispronouncing or misspelling it.

Identifying prefixes, suffixes and root words

Identifying commonly used **prefixes**, **suffixes** and **root words** can greatly assist in remembering their spelling. The word '**telephone**' referred to in the last paragraph is a good example of this. The **prefix** '**tele**' means distance while the root word '**phone**' means sound. By recognising this **common prefix**, the spelling of many other common words, such as '**television**' and '**telegraph**', becomes much easier. The recognition of the root word '**phone**', meaning sound, helps with the spelling of many other common words such as '**phonic**' and '**phoneme**'. The **suffix** '**ful**' is a good example of how early identification of the fact that it only has one 'l' as a suffix, but is spelt with two 'ls' when used **as a word on its own**, helps with the spelling of many words such as **peaceful**, **helpful**, **doubtful** and **bountiful**. An internet shortcut to a list of commonly used prefixes, suffixes and root words is on the CD-ROM.

⊙ (GO to Prefixes, Suffixes and Syllables Shortcut on CD-ROM)

You may like to use these as a base for building some new words and learning their spelling.

Using word families

Many words can be grouped into word families for easy recognition. Once you have identified a word as belonging to a particular family you will always recognise it and remember how to spell it. This is similar to the strategy mentioned previously, in that a **word family** can be identified by a particular prefix, suffix or root word. Once you have recognised that the words '**cycle**' and '**circle**' are derived from the same Greek word, it makes them much easier to remember and spell. Many dyslexic students have problems with words ending in '**er**' or '**or**' such as **builder** and **doctor**. To help you remember these, you might like to put them into two families where most of the '**er**' words refer to **trades** such as '**carpenter**', '**plumber**' and '**carrier**' and most of the '**or**' words to **professions** such as '**doctor**', '**solicitor**' and '**professor**'. This categorisation may well upset a lot of people like '**lecturers**' and '**teachers**', who certainly think they have professional roles, but like all spelling rules there are always exceptions and if grouping words into families helps you learn how to spell them, **that is all that is important**. Word families also help you not to confuse two **different words which sound similar** such as '**genius**' and '**ingenious**'. '**Genius**' comes from the **Latin** for '**creative principle**' and is in the word family with '**genus, genial, genital** and **genesis**'. On the other hand '**ingenious**' comes from the **Latin** for '**natural talent**'. There are some lists of word families on the CD-ROM if you wish to investigate this further.

A spelling programme

If you feel that your spelling requires a more intensive programme, you might like to try the Multisensory Spelling Programme for Priority Words (MUSP) which appears on the CD-ROM of *Making Dyslexia Work for You* by Vicki Goodwin and Bonita Thomson (2004). There are many spellcheckers and online dictionaries which students may find useful. One of the best is WordWeb which integrates well with Microsoft Word.

(GO to WordWeb shortcut on CD-ROM)

Others that can be considered are the Onelook Dictionary Search which suggests different definitions depending on the field of study, and Merriam Webster, which has the facility for the user to hear the word read.

In addition Microsoft Word contains features to help with spelling, such as AutoCorrect. This enables you to put in a list of words that you often misspell alongside the correct spelling and the program will automatically replace the red underlined incorrect word with the correct word. More simply, students should be aware of words which are underlined in red indicating a misspelling. To help with correction try putting your cursor on the word and clicking the right mouse button for some suggestions as to what you might mean.

Finally ClaroRead and Read&Write (see Chapter 4) contain predictive text facilities enabling you to type the first few letters of a word to obtain a list of possible words.

 case study

Harry was a science graduate doing his PGCE. He was very dyslexic but very able and very determined. He wanted to make sure that he could spell all the main words that he needed to spell in his science lessons and also be able to mark out errors in

(Continued)

(Continued)

his students' work. He made a list of all the words he wanted to learn and he worked on learning about 10–12 of them a week with his dyslexia tutor, using the 'Look-Say-Cover-Write-Check' method. This involves a spelling test at the end of the week and a dictation, with the words in context, at the end of a fortnight. If they were in his long-term memory at the end of the fortnight he felt he knew them, but periodically checked to see if he could spell them. In this way, learning a new set of 10–12 words a week and putting ones he found difficult or spelled incorrectly back into the learning list, he built up a repertoire of words he could spell and recognise competently and confidently.

As well as this he also wanted to improve his grammar. He used to read the paper on the train on the way to his dyslexia tutorial and started to mark out the content words – nouns, verbs, adjectives and adverbs – with different coloured highlighters. Over the year his ability to differentiate between the different parts of speech improved dramatically. He is now a confident science teacher.

case study

Sandra was an English graduate completing her teacher training. She knew she had to pass the spelling component of the basic skills testing. She had always been an avid reader but a poor speller, and knew that while you can read by orthographic methods (the shape of words, which are kept in the long-term memory), spelling is a very different matter, involving rules and recognition of phonemes (sounds) in words. She was determined to master spelling as an English teacher and systematically learnt rules for spelling, including all the exceptions. She had lists of 'demons' and made lists of word families such as those ending in 'or', 'er', 'ation', 'ition', 'ably' and 'ibly', etc., and also learnt all the variations of parts of speech from a root word such as; 'discriminate, discrimination, discriminating, discriminatingly, discriminately, indiscrininateness, indiscriminately', etc. She had all these lists available for constant visual observation, with the different endings colour coded, so they would go into her long-term memory. This worked very well; she passed the spelling test and went on to train English teachers and dyslexia tutors. Anything is possible. All you have to do is believe you can do it and work hard to achieve it.

Punctuation

Instructing the jury Judge Rutter got to the crux of the matter with superb clarity when he said you have to determine where the line has to be drawn between the force expected in a rugby match in which a person taking part is deemed to consent and that to which he is not deemed to consent.

Try reading the passage above. It shows why punctuation is important. Punctuation helps the reader to understand the writer's intended meaning, and, furthermore, allows the writer to be precise in expression.

The use of correct punctuation has been popularised through Lynne Truss's book *Eats, Shoots and Leaves*, which has become a bestseller. The title of the book is explained on the dust jacket. The phrase would be correctly punctuated **without the comma** if it is intended to describe the diet of a panda. As it stands it infers that the panda eats before shooting and then leaving. Another example was reported in a local paper on the problems of women giving up smoking, with the proposition: 'Women usually find it harder to give up smoking than men'. The reply followed: 'Who is trying to make women give up men, and will they please stop it?'

The most misused punctuation mark is the apostrophe. This is because people fail to realise that it only has two purposes, which are to show ownership or contraction.

Table 8.4 outlines the major functions of punctuation marks, with examples.

There are exercises on punctuation in the CD-ROM if you would like to see if you can put your new punctuation skills into practice.

(GO to Punctuation Exercises on CD-ROM)

There are several quick links to other information on grammar, spelling and punctuation on the CD-ROM.

Table 8.4   The major functions of punctuation marks

FULL STOP	1	To mark the end of a sentence:
		The man crept away without a word.
	2	To mark abbreviations:
		R.S.V.P., ref., cont.

(Continued)

Table 8.4   (Continued)

SEMICOLON	1	To separate independent main clauses in the same sentence when these aren't connected by a conjunction:
		The invasion began that night; it didn't last long.
	2	To act as a second grade of punctuation, in addition to the comma, in separating items in a series.
		The audience consisted of ten schoolgirls, each with notebook and pencil; two housewives, with restless children in their arms; and an eager-eyed dog, which wagged its tail through the entire performance.
COLON	1	To indicate that either examples or a restatement of what has just been said will follow:
		The fare must be simple: chicken, fresh salad and wine.
		The fare must be simple: things that take no time to prepare.
	2	To indicate that a quotation of direct speech is to follow.
		NB A comma may also be used for this.
		The stranger raised his voice: 'Is there anybody there?'
COMMA	1	To separate phrases and clauses which might otherwise, in the given arrangement of words, be misconstrued:
		A hundred metres below, the bridge was flooded.
		He was not cheerful, because he fell into the water.
		NB A comma marks off a phrase or clause which is the writer's added comment on the subject:
		The best policeman is the Irishman, who is large enough and vocal enough to inspire respect.
		Contrast the effect of leaving the comma out, which makes the same phrase or clause restrict the subject:
		The best policeman is the Irishman who is large enough and vocal enough to inspire respect.
	2	To set off an interposed phrase or clause:
		His father, the president of the club, appointed him.
		A trainee, however keen he is initially, won't want to continue at that pace.
	3	To separate items in a simple series:
		The audience consisted of ten schoolgirls, two housewives, a policeman and an eager-eyed dog.
APOSTROPHE	1	To mark possession:
		Max's approach, the novel's setting, the cars' horns
	2	To mark the omission of a letter or letters:
		couldn't, they're, I'm tired
QUESTION MARK		To mark a question:
		How goes it?

EXCLAMATION MARK	1	To mark an exclamation:
		Heaven help us!
	2	To mark a command:
		Let my people go!
QUOTATION MARKS (Inverted Commas)	1	To enclose actual words spoken:
		He said: 'I'm not coming.'
	2	To enclose a quotation of any kind:
		Few people I've met have such a 'do or die' attitude.
	3	To mark foreign words or phrases, or words or phrases under discussion:
		'carabinieri', 'bête noire', the term 'democracy'
		NB A common alternative practice is just to underline such words or phrases.
DASH	1	To indicate a break in the grammar of the main sentence:
		He sang loudly – I found him far too loud – and with little sensitivity.
	2	NB Brackets are an alternative way of marking off an interjected, explanatory or qualifying remark.
		He sang loudly (I found him far too loud) and with little sensitivity.
		To show that what follows is a summary addition to the sentence:
		The applicant shows energy and initiative – both essential to the task.

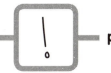 **points to remember**

- Make sure that all your sentences contain a subject and a verb which agrees with the subject (sentence kernel).
- Keep your sentences short. A sentence that runs on over two lines is usually too long.
- You CAN learn to spell words which you want to learn to spell by using a variety of strategies.
- Make sure that your sentences make sense and say what you intend them to say by using correct punctuation.

CD-ROM Contents

Please go to the CD-ROM accompanying this book to find the following documents:

Conjunctive Adverbs	Word Document
English Grammar Card	PDF

Look-Say-Cover-Write-Check Template	Word Document
More Pronouns	Word Document
Punctuation Exercises	Word Document

Please go to the CD-ROM accompanying this book to find links to the following:

BBC Skillswise
Fifty Writing Tools for Journalists
Grammar and Punctuation Rules
Grammar Girl's Quick and Dirty Tips for Better Writing
Grammarama
Most Difficult Words to Spell
Prefixes, Suffixes and Syllables
Punctuation Made Simple
Word Families
WordWeb

9

Improving Mathematics Skills and Using Statistics

Judith Cattermole and John Brennan

developmental objectives

This chapter:

- outlines strategies using concrete materials to help you overcome maths problems
- outlines the two main (cognitive) approaches to tackling maths problems (namely the 'grasshopper' and 'inchworm' approaches)
- demystifies the symbolic language of maths
- suggests ways of learning formulae, if necessary
- suggests strategies for overcoming problems with fractions including templates of concrete material to use (CD-ROM)
- suggests strategies for overcoming problems with decimals (CD-ROM)
- suggests strategies for overcoming problems with statistics including templates of concrete material to use (CD-ROM).

If you have sometimes experienced problems with arithmetic or working with numbers then you may find this chapter helpful; especially if your course work requires an ability to work with **fractions, mathematical formulae, decimals and statistics**. In this chapter you will find some strategies that have worked with other students who have had similar problems. It will concentrate on using **concrete materials and exercises**, which have been helpful for students in overcoming their problems.

It is not unusual for dyslexic students to experience difficulties with the mathematical content of their course but just as there are ways of helping you with other study skills, there are strategies you can use to help you solve maths problems. According to Vicki Goodman and Bonita Thomson (2004), about 60% of dyslexic people have some difficulties with maths but these are often to do with *procedures and remembering the order in which the operations should be undertaken* rather than the mathematical concepts.

Thinking (cognitive) and learning styles

In maths it has been customary to refer to the two main cognitive approaches to problem solving as the **inchworm** and the **grasshopper approaches** (Chinn and Ashcroft,1998). These are simply alternate ways of describing a more **holistic** (grasshopper) approach or a more **analytical** (inchworm) approach. You may have used the questionnaire in Chapter 2 to help you to think about your own cognitive and learning style. The three learning styles, namely **visual**, **auditory** and **kinaesthetic,** can also be applied to learning mathematical concepts and many of the concrete methods suggested here are a combination of both visual and kinaesthetic styles. You should use the information you gained in Chapter 2 to adapt the advice and tips in this chapter to suit your own cognitive and learning style. In addition to this and in the same way that you may have a preferred approach for dealing with words and letters, you may have a preferred approach for solving mathematical problems. The two main types are described below.

Inchworms typically:

- focus on the details
- work methodically
- check answers by going through their working from the beginning
- follow instructions.

Grasshoppers, on the other hand:

- take an overview of the whole problem
- will probably give an intuitive answer
- work back from their answer to check if it is correct
- adjust numbers to make the calculation easier.

You may not clearly fall into one category or the other and feel that **you use different methods to solve different problems**. **Choosing a method of working to suit the task** can be helpful and many people work in this way. If you are having difficulties with a mathematical problem and if you feel that you are working like an inchworm or a grasshopper it might be helpful to try using different techniques and approach. Neither method is right or wrong but one can be more helpful than the other for solving different problems.

Useful tips

Wherever possible use **concrete materials** to help you understand processes and concepts. Typical things that students use are; paper, string, coins, buttons, and even sweets and chocolate bars (this has the advantage of added treat or reward value, but the disadvantage that you might gain weight). Doing things physically can help you to understand concepts and theories. We shall go into this in more detail in the section on fractions.

Use squared paper for calculations: this will help you to:

- line up numbers, symbols and decimal points vertically and horizontally
- draw charts, tables and diagrams neatly
- calculate areas.

Use a **calculator** wherever possible but always try to estimate your answer first, so you know if you have approximately the right answer on your calculator. Choose a calculator with a large display and keys, which are easy to press. Do the calculation twice to check if you have the right answer.

Language of maths

Understand the **language of maths**. One symbol can be used to express different everyday words:

Common symbols	
Symbol	**Words**
=	equals, is the same as, equivalent to
+	add, sum, and, plus, total
−	minus, subtract, take away
×	times, multiply, of
÷	divide, goes into, split, share, per
<	is less than
>	is more than, is greater than
Advanced symbols	
n^x	means the number n is 'raised to the power x'. So 6^2 means 6×6 (= 36) and 2^3 means $2 \times 2 \times 2$ (= 8). The power of 2 is called 'squared' (6^2 is 6 squared) and the power of 3 is called 'cubed' (2^3 is 2 cubed)
$\sqrt{}$	means 'square root'. This is the number which squared equals the number after the sign. So $\sqrt{n}$ is the number m for which $m \times m = n$. For example $\sqrt{25}$ is 5 because $5 \times 5 = 25$
Σ	sum of all the numbers
σ	measures the distribution or spread of the data

Formulae are ways of expressing mathematical relationships or rules. They use symbols and letters instead of words, for example:

$$E = mc^2$$

Energy is equal to mass times **speed of light squared**

E	=	m	(×)	c	2

Notice that in formulae using symbols the times (×) sign is not included.

Not all universities and colleges require students to remember formula and will give them to you as part of the exam questions. Others will allow students with dyslexia to take designated help sheets into exams. Find out what your university or college allows you to do rather than using valuable study time in trying to remember something that you don't need to.

Example formulae – converting Centigrade to Fahrenheit

The relationship between temperatures measured in degrees Centigrade (Tc) and degrees Fahrenheit (Tf) is given by the formula:

$$9Tc = 5(Tf - 32)$$

9 times **Centigrade** is equal to **5** times
Opening Brackets Fahrenheit less **32 Closing Brackets**

9	×	Tc	=	5	×
(		Tf	–	32	)

This formula has something new, namely brackets. Brackets are used in mathematics to indicate the order in which operations (adding, subtracting, multiplying, etc.) are performed. If there are multiple operations in a calculation the order in which they are done will often affect the result.

In order to be clear, rules and procedures have been agreed to define the order of operations in formulae. It is essential to do the operations in the correct order to get the right answer:

- Do things in brackets first.
  - ✓ $7 \times (4 + 3)$ $= 7 \times 7$ $= \mathbf{49}$ ☺
  - ✗ $7 \times (4 + 3)$ $= 28 + 3 = \mathbf{31}$ (wrong ☹)

- Powers and roots before multiply, divide, add or subtract.
  - ✓ 5×2^2 $= 5 \times 4$ $= \mathbf{20}$ ☺
  - ✗ 5×2^2 $= 10^2$ $= \mathbf{100}$ (wrong ☹)

- Multiply or divide before you add or subtract.
  - ✓ $3 + 4 \times 5$ $= 3 + 20 = \mathbf{23}$ ☺
  - ✗ $3 + 4 \times 5$ $= 7 \times 5$ $= \mathbf{35}$ (wrong ☹)

- Otherwise just go left to right.
  - ✓ $30 \div 5 \times 3$ $= 6 \times 3$ $= \mathbf{18}$ ☺
  - ✗ $30 \div 5 \times 3$ $= 30 \div 15 = \mathbf{2}$ (wrong ☹)

These rules can be remembered through the acronym BODMAS (see Figure 9.1.)!

Example formulae – relationship between distance, time and speed

The relationship between distance (D), time (T) and speed (S) can be presented graphically by the triangle:

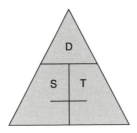

Figure 9.1   BODMAS

B   Brackets first
O   Orders (i.e. powers and square roots, etc.)
DM   Division and Multiplication (left-to-right)
AS   Addition and Subtraction (left-to-right)

This is intended to show that:

Distance (D) = Speed (S) × Time (T)
Speed (S) = Distance (D) ÷ Time (T)
Time (T) = Distance (D) ÷ Speed (S)

Note that these equations are not independent; any two can be derived from the third. This can be demonstrated by thinking of an equation with an = sign as an old-fashioned beam balance, which, unlike the illustration is in balance. The beam will remain in balance if what is added or subtracted from one side is added or subtracted from the other. So it is with equations; whatever (adding something, subtracting something, multiplying by something or dividing by something) one does to one side of the equation must be done to the other. Taking the first distance equation:

Distance (D) = Speed (S) × Time (T)

or

$D = S \times T$

dividing both sides by T would give:

$D \div T = (S \times T) \div T$

which is:

$D \div T = S \times (T \times T)$

which is:

$D \div T = S$

rearranging gives the 2nd equation:

$S = D \div T$

Most equations, such as these, always require that the units used are consistent. In the United Kingdom we might use miles for distance and hours for time to express the speed of a car journey as miles per hour; in modern countries using the metric system one would use kilometres for distance and hours for time to express speed as kilometres per hour. In a different context, such as measuring the speed of a glacier, one could use centimetres for distance and years for time. Remember that the units on one side of an equation must always be the same as those on the other side.

If you need to remember formula:

- Write them in a **note book** in a way that is helpful to you. For example by using **colour** or **different thickness** of pens.
- Write the formula out in words, for example:

Volume   equals   length   **times**   breadth   times   height
    V   **=**   **l**   (×)   **b**   (×)   **h**

- Use **mnemonics** containing words that are significant to you or something you find amusing. Anything will do as long as you find it easy to remember.

Anne is a single mother of two toddlers and remembered the Energy formula of the start of this section as:

Exhaustion   is the same as   mother times children (2)

     E   =   m   (×)   c   2

- **Seek help**: If you are receiving tutorial support make sure that your tutor knows that you have problems with numbers. Some universities and colleges offer specialist numeracy help either to groups of students or individuals. Find out if you are entitled to this type of help.
- **Search the internet**. There are websites which offer help to adults with dyslexia and numeracy difficulties; two of the best are the
  - ○ BBC Skillswise support
  - ○ DfES Adult Numeracy core curriculum.

The Dyscalculia and Dyslexia Interest Group based at Loughborough University provides an opportunity for exchange of information for students and tutors about issues of studying maths in higher education for students from a variety of backgrounds including dyslexic students.

Understanding fractions

Many students find understanding fractions difficult so here are some ways of using the above techniques which you could find helpful. If they don't work for you then use your imagination to adapt them to suit your own needs and learning style.

Try this technique of folding paper. It might be easier if you use squared paper which will give you some lines to use for folding.

After you have folded the paper once along the middle you will have two equal parts (two halves), which make one whole. The words **one half** are written numerically as a fraction:

$$\frac{1}{2}$$

You can write this fraction on each piece of paper:

Fold line

Notice that:

- The number under the line tells you how many pieces make a whole one: **the denominator.**
- The number on top of the line tells you how many pieces in that fraction: **the numerator.**

(It is easy to remember: **d**enominator and **d**own start with same letter.)

Fold the paper along the original fold line and then fold it in half again. Open it out. You will now have four pieces (four quarters). The words one quarter are written numerically as a fraction:

$$\frac{1}{4}$$

You can write this fraction on each piece of paper:

$\frac{1}{4}$	$\frac{1}{4}$	$\frac{1}{4}$	$\frac{1}{4}$
Fold line	Fold line	Fold line	

You can carry on folding the same piece of paper for more fractions, which will give you:

Eight pieces:

$\frac{1}{8}$	$\frac{1}{8}$	$\frac{1}{8}$	$\frac{1}{8}$
$\frac{1}{8}$	$\frac{1}{8}$	$\frac{1}{8}$	$\frac{1}{8}$

Take another piece of squared paper and this time fold it into three equal pieces to give you thirds:

$$\frac{1}{3}$$

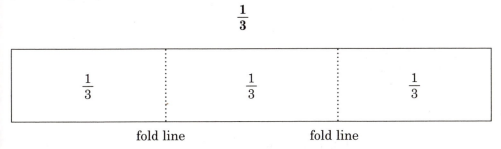

$\frac{1}{3}$	$\frac{1}{3}$	$\frac{1}{3}$
fold line	fold line	

Write the correct fraction in each piece. If you folded the paper again how many pieces would there be?

Alternative approaches

Using colour

Some students find folding the paper fiddly and prefer a different approach using different colours to represent different fractions.

You can try using one piece of grey paper to represent the whole one on which you can lay differently coloured segments of paper to represent, halves, quarters, eighths, thirds, sixths, fifths and tenths.

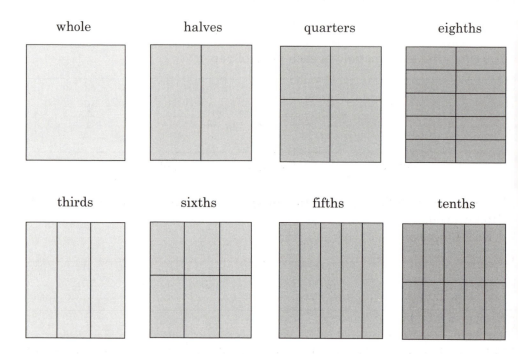

You can **colour code** the different segments to demonstrate the different 'fraction families' and to help you remember the relationship between:

- halves, quarters and eighths
- thirds and sixths
- fifths and tenths.

Using a fraction wall

An alternative approach is to use the fraction wall, which is on the CD-ROM. This combines elements of the folding and colour techniques.

Not all these methods will be suitable for everyone; choose the one that works best for you or, even better, use your own ideas to adapt these methods or make up your own.

On the CD-ROM you will also find some help sheets that explain how to make calculations using fractions. These are intended to be used only as a reminder and backup learning aids and not as a replacement for tactile, visual and verbal techniques you may want to try out for yourself.

Decimals

Like fractions, decimals are used to represent parts of things. A decimal number uses a decimal point (a dot) to separate whole things (integers) on the left from parts of things (fractions) on the right.

Examples	$\frac{1}{2}$ = 0.5	$\frac{1}{3}$ = 0.3333	A decimal can be seen as a fraction of tenths, hundreds, thousands and so on.
	$\frac{1}{4}$ = 0.25		So 0.25 is $\frac{25}{100}$
	$\frac{1}{8}$ = 0.125	$\frac{2}{3}$ = 0.6667	
	$\frac{5}{8}$ = 0.625		

Thus if you see a decimal such as 0.216 this means there are:

Two tenths + one hundredths + 6 thousandths

Or:

$$\frac{2}{10} + \frac{1}{100} + \frac{6}{1000}$$

Remember the whole numbers on the left of the decimal point get larger as they move away from the decimal point, but the numbers on the right get smaller.

hundreds   tens   units   tenths   hundredths   thousandths

larger← 153.216 →Smaller

Test yourself

Put the following decimal numbers in sequence starting with the smallest number first and ending with the largest:

100.6   99.16   9.3   100.59   100.635   9.08   31.5   31.49

Fill in the missing numbers in each sequence

3.97   3.98   3.99   _____

24.97   24.98   24.99   _____   25.01   25.02   25.03

On the CD-ROM there are some help sheets which explain in more detail how to do decimal calculations.

case study for fractions

Paul was a foundation year business studies student who described himself as a failure because he was struggling with the mathematical content of his course. He was particularly concerned about his inability to understand the concept of fractions and decimals. He felt that this was probably due to his dyslexia and his inability to concentrate for extended periods of time. He also said that figures (numbers) often became blurry and he lost his place when looking at a series of numbers. Because of his past failures in maths he said that he felt like giving up before he started with some course work questions that included fractions and decimals because he found them so difficult to understand.

Paul said that 'I like to visualise things in my head so I can see the whole picture of the problem'. When he was presented with a problem he would give an estimated trial answer and then work backwards to see if he was right. He did not like to write things down but worked things out mentally in his head. Paul said that he liked the challenge that this presented and, that writing things out was boring and that seeing the numbers and symbols on the page muddled him up. He did like to work with concrete materials but found the folding of paper method 'fiddly and time consuming', but he did enjoy working with different coloured paper as this was 'more exciting and visual'.

He also liked the opportunity to add and take away different pieces of paper and immediately saw that if he took away, for example one quarter from three quarters which were laid over the grey whole one, he was left with two quarters, which was equal to half of the whole one. He liked approaching this as a puzzle and working out which pieces he could use.

points to remember

- Use concrete materials as a starting point to help you to understand number concepts and processes.
- Try to use your own learning styles to develop techniques that will help you.
- Be prepared to progress at a rate which suits you.

- Use materials that appeal to your own needs and be prepared to adapt them if necessary.
- Don't be surprised if your progress and development is not regular and be prepared for revision periods.
- Try out different methods and techniques, especially if you seem to be working at either end of the grasshopper–inchworm continuum.
- Be prepared to seek or ask for more expert help if this is appropriate.

Statistics

Statistics is a range of techniques for gathering, organising, analysing and presenting quantitative data (Brown and Saunders, 2008). It attempts to maximise the interpretation, understanding and use of 'raw' data; it tries, if you will, to enable one to see 'the wood for the trees' where numbers are concerned. Statistics is used by those studying the social sciences, medicine, psychology and business, amongst other subjects.

In the following section you can see how a subject like statistics, which many dyslexic students find very difficult, can become more accessible with the use of colour, visual representations and concrete examples. The basic statistical concepts of **mean**, **median**, **mode** and **distribution** are demonstrated through these methods.

Mean, median and mode

A student measured the heights of 11 university students. The results were arranged in increasing order (rank order) – see Figure 9.2.

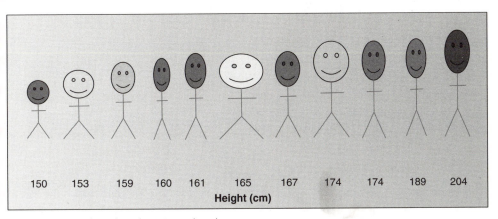

| 150 | 153 | 159 | 160 | 161 | 165 | 167 | 174 | 174 | 189 | 204 |

Height (cm)

Figure 9.2   Heights of students in rank order

There are three different ways of thinking about an average of a set of numbers:

- mean (arithmetic average) written as $\bar{x}$
- median (middle number)
- mode (most frequent).

Mean

The mean, or arithmetic mean (shown in Figure 9.3), is written as:

$$\bar{x} = \Sigma\, \chi/n$$

Where:

Σ (sigma) the sum of the sample (all the values added together)

n the number of samples (in this example $n = 11$ people)

χ the value of the sample (the number)

$$\Sigma\chi/n \;=\; \frac{150+153+159+160+161+165+167+174+174+189+204}{11}$$

$\bar{x}$ 168.73

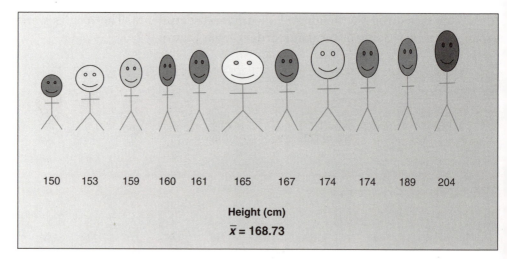

Figure 9.3   Mean height of students

Taking another set of numbers: 40, 41, 55, 55, 60, 65

The mean is: $\bar{x} = \dfrac{40+41+55+55+60+65}{6}$

$$= 52.66$$

In this case, because of the two small readings, the mean is smaller than most of the numbers in the sample.

Median

The median of a group is the middle number in a list when arranged in rank order. In the student heights sample, the median is the 6th number (see Figure 9.4).

This works for odd numbers, but if the sample is even then the median is taken as the arithmetic mean of the middle two numbers.

For example, given the set:

1, 1, 2, 3, 4, 5, 6, 7.

The median is $\dfrac{3+4}{2} = 3.5$

By contrast the mean is $\bar{x} = 3.63$

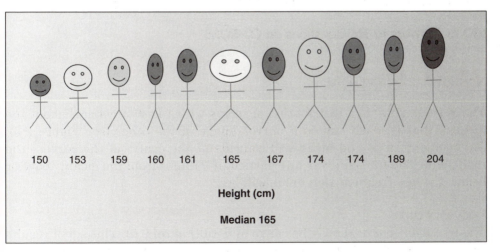

| 150 | 153 | 159 | 160 | 161 | 165 | 167 | 174 | 174 | 189 | 204 |

Height (cm)

Median 165

Figure 9.4   Median height of students

Mode

The mode is the measurement that occurs the greatest number of times. In the case of the student heights, the mode is 174.

Sometimes there may be several modal values in a set of data.

In the set:

46, 48, 50, 50, 51, 51, 51, 52, 53, 53, 53

There are two modal values; 51 and 53

The median of this set is 51

While the mean $\bar{x} = \dfrac{46+48+50+50+51+51+52+53+53+53}{11}$

$= 50.73$

Problems

Rank the following numbers then calculate the mean, median and mode.

1 **23, 45, 54, 45, 67, 45, 56, 67, 34**
2 **34, 45, 45, 23, 34, 45, 45, 67, 65, 43**
3 **2, 4, 5, 7, 2, 4, 3, 7, 5**
4 **1, 4, 6, 4, 8, 7, 6, 5, 4, 5**

The answers can be found on the CD-ROM.

(GO to Answers to 3M Questions on CD-ROM)

Normal distribution data

The normal curve is a distribution of scores which is symmetrical about the mean – that is, each side is a mirror image of the other (see Figure 9.5). The median, mode and mean will coincide at the centre of the curve – the high point. The further away any particular value is from the mean, above or below, the less frequent that value will be.

Frequency curve

The frequency curve shows the range of data (Figure 9.6). This set of results show that the distribution is not symmetrical and the data are positively skewed (skewed to the left) (see Figure 9.7). This indicates that the lower values have a higher frequency, very few tall people.

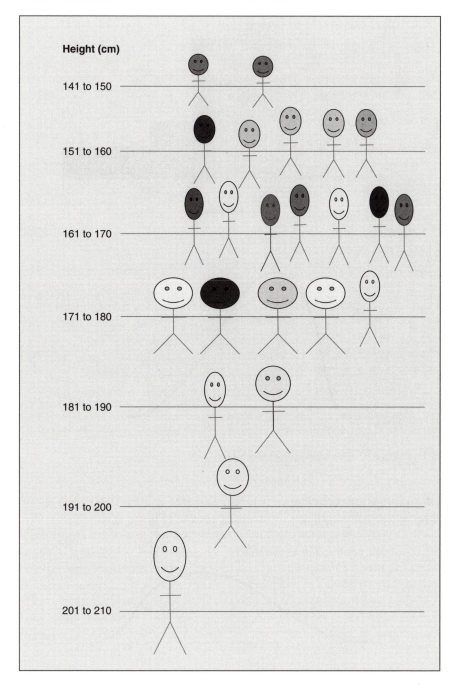

Figure 9.5   Heights of students in a lecture theatre showing normal distribution

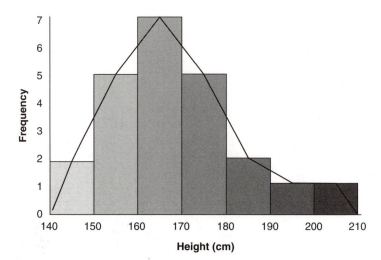

Figure 9.6   Frequency curve

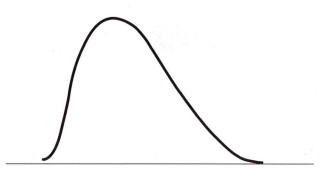

Figure 9.7   Frequency curve – positively skewed

If the frequency curve is negatively skewed (skewed to the right) then there would be more tall people and few short people (Figure 9.8).

Figure 9.8   Frequency curve – negatively skewed

If the frequency curve is symmetrical then there is a normal distribution of heights with equal amounts of tall and short people (Figure 9.9).

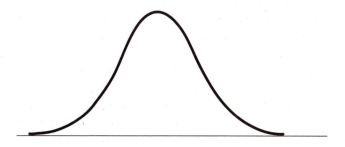

Figure 9.9   Frequency curve – normal and symmetrical

The range

The range is the difference between the highest number and the lowest number. In the case of the students' heights the range is:

$$210 - 140 = 70$$

For different sets of data the mean and the range could be the same, yet the distribution of the data could be completely different.

The standard deviation

The **standard deviation is often used to measure the distribution or spread of the data**. For a reasonably symmetrical and bell shaped set of data like the one above, **one standard deviation** each side of the mean will include roughly **68%** of the data and **two standard deviations** each side will include roughly **95%** of the data. Therefore the size of the standard deviation is a measure of the spread of the data. If somebody says that the data has a **small standard deviation**, they mean that a lot of the **data is grouped closely around the mean**, i.e. there are lots of people of about the same height. If it has a large standard deviation then there is obviously a wide range of heights in the group.

Inferential statistics

So far we have been covering techniques for describing a set of data; this branch of statistics is known as 'Descriptive Statistics'. Although universities are interested in descriptions and students will gain credit for good descriptions of data, they are more interested in analysis. Students will be required to make inferences from data collected in projects or dissertations. Equally students must be able to review and evaluate the inferences drawn by others. This branch of statistics is known as 'Inferential (analytical) Statistics'.

Statistics can never prove a premise completely; the best they can do is provide strong support for an hypothesis, inference or conclusion. Evaluating this support is a form of critical analysis. Discussion of the statistical tests used to support an inference drawn from a sample is beyond the scope of this book, but there are many resources on the web; links to some of these are on the CD-ROM. Continue to use colour, visual representations and concrete examples to make sense of terms such as *probability, confidence, correlation* and *coefficient of determination*.

points to remember

- There are three possible ways of obtaining the averages from data, after you have arranged them into rank order (rank order = increasing value, e.g. 1, 2, 3, ...7, 8, 9, 10...):
  o Mean is the average value.
  o Median is the middle number.
  o Mode is the number which comes up the most times, and can be more than one number.
- The size of the standard deviation gives you an idea of the spread of the sample.

further resources

If you have found this chapter helpful you might also find other books and websites helpful. As a start you could try:

Dyslexia at College by D.G. Gilroy and T.R. Miles (1996) which has a useful chapter on algebra and statistics.

Statistics for the Terrified. Concept Stew Ltd – Available from: www.conceptstew.co.uk/PAGES/home.html

www.mathsisfun.com

Making Dyslexia Work for You, by Vicki Goodwin and Bonita Thomson (2004), which gives lots of helpful tips for adult dyslexic people and includes a chapter on handling numbers.

Dealing with Statistics: What You Need to Know, by R.B. Brown and M.Saunders (2008), Open University Press, Maidenhead.

CD-ROM Contents

Please go to the CD-ROM accompanying this book to find the following documents:

Adding and Subtracting Fractions	Word Document
Answers to 3M Questions	Word Document
Calculating with Decimals	Word Document
Fraction Walls	Word Document
Fractions	Word Document
Is This a True Dice?	Excel Worksheet
Multiplying Fractions	Word Document
Normal Distribution	PNG Image
PASW Statistics	PDF
Statistics and Measurement Using OpenStat	Word Document
Test Yourself Answers	Word Document
Times Table	Excel Worksheet
Understanding Decimals	Word Document
Understanding Fractions – Folding Paper Method	Word Document
Understanding Fractions – Using Colour	Word Document

Please go to the CD-ROM accompanying this book to find links to the following:

BBC GCSE Bitesize Maths
BBC Skillswise
Calculus
Centre for Innovation in Mathematics Teaching
Fundamental Statistics for the Behavioural Sciences
GCSE Guide
How to Convert Units of Measurement
Karl Wuensch's Statistical Help Page
Manipula Math

Math2
Mathematics – Awesome Library
Mathtutor
Prime Numbers
Statistics for the Terrified
Web Pages that Perform Statistical Calculations!

10

Examination Techniques

Sandra Hargreaves

developmental objectives

When preparing for examinations:

- adopt the right mindset
- make all the appropriate preparations for your examinations well in advance
- plan your revision and your exam timetables
- revise for your examinations according to your cognitive and learning style
- practise sample examination questions under timed conditions.

This chapter also looks at the **day before** the exam and gives you tips on sitting examinations. There is also some useful advice on how to cope during the examination period.

Adopting the right mindset

Many dyslexic students would prefer to choose courses that do not contain examinations, as they require recall and written expression under time pressure. These activities can cause dyslexic students big problems as they require good working memory and written expression. You may also wish to discuss alternative methods of assessment (such as giving a presentation) with your tutor or the dyslexia coordinator at your college.

If, however, you have to do exams, it is not all doom and gloom. Reasons to love exams include:

- Compared to coursework you need less in-depth research and reading.
- You don't have to write out full references.
- You are allowed more leeway with minor grammatical errors, spellings and forgotten details – though handwriting must stay legible!
- This is your chance to prove what you have learnt.
- You will feel great when you have done them to the best of your ability.
- They are over and done with quickly.

You need to prepare yourself well in advance. Leaving revision until the last moment and 'cramming' only increases your anxiety. Anxiety causes lack of sleep and poor recall of what you have managed to put into your long-term memory. **The key for dyslexic students is to ensure that all the material you need for examinations is in your long-term memory** where you can draw on it to answer the questions you will be given. With the additional time you are given, as a dyslexic student, for reading and processing the questions and recalling the information you have learned, there should be nothing to make you anxious.

Making administrative preparations

Most colleges have strict cut-off dates for notifying the assessment unit of the special provisions to which you are entitled. Every institution will have slightly different arrangements, and it is your responsibility to ensure that the arrangements are in place for you well before every examination period. **You must not assume that just because you have notified the university or college of your dyslexia that the arrangements will be made.** All students have specific arrangements designed to help them overcome their particular weaknesses. All dyslexic students are given extra time so long as they have proven their dyslexia to the institution. The amount of time, however, may vary between students. Some students prefer to use word processors, and some amanuenses (scribes). Others will require readers, or examination papers in different colours or printed in larger font. **Whatever your needs, they should appear in your Needs Assessment and must be agreed with the dyslexia coordinator in the institution you attend.** If your institution provides stickers or memos for you to put on your papers to alert the markers to your dyslexia, don't forget to take them with you to the exam.

Many colleges and universities also expect students to notify the assessment unit about the modules they are taking in each exam period so that the examination arrangements, which have to be made with the dyslexia coordinator, can be put into place. **Check what your institution expects**.

Planning your revision and your exam timetables

Once all of the administrative arrangements are planned you can begin on the real business of examination revision. **The first step is to write a list of what you need to revise**.

(GO to Revision List on CD-ROM)

The list of assignments which you prepared at the beginning of the term outlined in Chapter 1 can be modified for this purpose. A blank template is available on the CD-ROM. **Once you know the extent of your revision, you can draw up a revision timetable and an examination timetable**, which again can be based on the timetables described in Chapter 1. Blank templates are also available on the CD-ROM.

(GO to Revision Timetable on CD-ROM)

Revision timetable

Make sure when you compile your revision timetable that it reflects the requirements of the examination timetable. Be careful that you do not fall into obvious traps such as spending all your time on revising for the first examination and fail to leave time for subsequent examinations.

With your revision timetable, put down realistic time slots for revision and vary your topics across each day. A lot has been written on the subject of attention span but remember that **30–40 minutes of uninterrupted attention** on revision is about as much as the mind can absorb. You should then have a break. Either at the end of the revision session or before starting another session, **recall what you have learnt in the previous session**.

(GO to Exam Timetable on CD-ROM)

Exam timetable

Double check, when compiling your examination timetable, that you:

- Note the correct date for each examination.
- Check the time of each examination.

- Know where you are to sit each exam. Many students have destroyed all their preparation in a few moments by going to the wrong examination room, or even the wrong building. Colleges are large and sometimes rambling institutions. During examination periods every available room is often in use, and students frequently have to sit examinations in rooms where they have never been before. It is imperative to go and find the room in which you will be doing the examination well before you have to sit for the paper.

Check with your friends to see that they have the same information. Being in the wrong place or at the wrong time is a costly error, as you will then have to resit the examination.

The final preparations, and those which should ensure that you will be successful, are **knowing the location of the room** and going in to take the examination **well rested, well fed, calm and confident**.

Be good to yourself

It is important that you allocate time for relaxation, exercise and plenty of sleep in both the revision timetable and the examination timetable itself.

- Drink plenty of water for optimum brain vitality.
- Eat healthily and at regular intervals. Keep a regular, relaxed routine. Consume caffeine and cigarettes in moderation (if you have to!).
- Build in exercise and movement; it may help you sleep well at night.
- Perhaps revise with like-minded friends. Avoid the ones that make you nervous or undermine your confidence.
- Use a relaxation technique that you use every day when you are working well. There are a variety of relaxation techniques which can be used, including yoga, meditation and Brain Gym® (Paul Dennison – see 'References and Further reading').
- Work on staying positive.
- Reward yourself for sticking to your revision schedule, so that you are in peak performance for the big day.

Revising according to your thinking and learning style

Remember, when you begin to revise, look at course module outlines, reread key texts and lecture notes and make good notes (see Chapter 3). You should start as soon as possible, keeping to your revision timetable.

Much of what was covered in Chapter 2 applies to examination revision. You might like to go back and review that chapter before proceeding with your revision. Look at the different learning strategies (Figures 2.2, 2.3, 2.4 and 2.5) to see which revision techniques you wish to use. If you have a **holistic cognitive style, you may wish to prepare an overview of a whole topic** before revising sections of it. This can be done using a concept map or spider diagram. If you are more **analytical, you may wish to learn individual sections and build towards the 'big picture'** of the topic you are covering.

Memory

Many students with dyslexia are scared of exams because they have, or think they have, a poor memory and fear they are unable to recall anything they have revised. Guess what, we all have poor memories for the sort of things needed in exams: names, dates or numbers. This is what Joshua Foer, who went on to win the USA Memory Championship, had to say:

> My memory was average, at best. Among the things I regularly forgot: where I put my car keys (and where I put my car, for that matter); the food in the oven; that it's 'its' and not 'it's'; my girlfriend's birthday, our anniversary, Valentine's Day; my friends' phone numbers; why I just opened the fridge. (Foer, 2011)

So how did he do it? **By training his memory** using techniques, some of which date back to the 5th century BC. The essential point of all memory techniques is to transform the kinds of memories we are not very good at, into the kinds of memories our brains were built for. Using your thinking and learning style to **associate** what you want to remember with places (loci in Latin, hence the term for this technique 'Method of Loci' or **'memory palace'**) you are intimately familiar with. These places can be actual places, such as your home or your childhood home, or conceptual places such as a journey on the train or around your garden, or based around stories you make up and clothes in your wardrobe.

Visual revision techniques

- Create **posters** to display around the room using **bright colours** and a **large font** to make the layout clear and eye-catching (see Stefan's case study below).
- **Concept maps** are particularly useful for exam revision. Create new maps for each topic you are revising.
- Use **rooms** in your house for different subjects or topics. When you are trying to recall the information elsewhere, visualise yourself in the room to trigger your memory.

- Use **visual memory pegs** to learn lists of items, dates or terminology. Link the visual peg for the number with the item you are learning.
- Use **index cards**, either with points for each topic written in bullets or with a question on one side and points for the answer on the other. It is a good idea to **colour code** your index cards so that you have different coloured cards for each subject or topic.

Auditory revision techniques

- Use **mnemonics** to recall information, such as factual terms and material or even how to spell a word.
- Create **acronyms** to synthesise a set of data, a list of terms or a set of topics into one word (doesn't need to be a real word) so that when you recall it in the examination you can remember all the information attached to it (see Doris's case study below).
- Use **auditory memory pegs** to learn lists of items, dates or terminology.
- Read your revision cards aloud or ask a friend or family member to ask you questions so that you can explain the information you are trying to understand to them.
- **Record the points** you are revising on a mini-disk or other digital recording device. Play them back when you are doing something else like housework or travelling on the train.
- **Discuss your work** with a friend. You could get together with a classmate and compare your understanding of certain concepts or topics, which of course will help them too.

Kinaesthetic revision techniques

- Compile study notes on a mini-disk and listen to them while walking, cycling or jogging.
- Write out your notes a few times, **condensing them down to just a few key words** that will trigger your memory of the subject.
- Use **highlighter pens to colour code** different topics or **draw pictures** to relate to the different topics.
- If your assessment includes a presentation, **practise your presentation** in front of someone you know, in the mirror or on video.
- If your assessment includes a practical component, use **role play** as an effective way of putting your knowledge into practice, before the practical examination.

Look at the following case studies. The first is a comment by **a multi-sensory learner**, Stefan, who uses **visual techniques** in the production of **posters** and **index cards**, combined with the **auditory techniques** of **rehearsing the contents of the cards** aloud in front of the mirror or to family members. **Kinaesthetic methods** are also used in **rewriting and condensing notes**.

stefan's case study – using multi-sensory techniques

When I revise, I find a combination of two approaches is the most effective. In the longer-term lead up to an exam (three or so weeks), I try to write all those important details which are hard to remember (such as lists, quotes, timelines and diagrams) onto posters. I usually just use A4 plain paper, and I make them in lots of eye-catching colours on the computer. With one wall of my bedroom dedicated to each subject (at A2, this means that you get one free wall!), it is a really non-stressed way to revise, since every time I am in my room I'm just able to 'soak it up' without much effort on my part. I can revise by staring at my wall.

The other way I revise is to make notes on index cards. Each subject has its own colour of card (blue for History, yellow for Music, pink for Religious Studies) and I try to use a few different colours of biro for points, quotes and headings. When I've written a set of notes, I write them all out again but this time trying to condense them. Going through this seemingly endless 'condensation' process is what gets it drilled into my mind. The other bonus is that I can always carry them around in my pocket and have a look at them whenever I'm waiting for a train, or any other time I get a spare moment. It's good to see everything you have to know down on a few cards, rather than on millions of scrappy sheets in a folder.

The second case study is a comment by a **visual** and **auditory** learner. Note how Doris uses visual methods to create the Mind Map™ but auditory methods in the form of mnemonics to recall it.

case study – exam mind map™ created by doris

This Mind Map™ (Figure 10.1) is specifically related to memory strategies and recall. There are five traits that I needed to memorise with a number of factors related to each of those traits. NEO AGRI CONSCIENTIOUSNESS is a mnemonic for the five traits. The more connections I make with a piece of information, the easier it is to recall and the connection I made here was that new agriculture is conscientious.

The same goes for AGREEABLENESS. I saw a film called *I Am Sam* in which Sean Penn plays a person who has learning difficulties who is fighting for custody of his daughter and embodies the factors of the traits in the character he is playing. If I split this Mind

(Continued)

(Continued)

Map™ over three pages so that when printed the Mind Map™ was easy to see, I would have a number at the top of the page to indicate how many sections I would have on each page. This would then give me a number I could memorise, so if I had two sections on each page, the number would be 222. So in an exam I would remember the number, visualise the pictures and then the picture would prompt the mnemonic.

Practising sample examination questions under timed conditions

It is crucial to obtain a **bank of sample questions or past examination papers** during the revision period. When you feel that you have revised your work as well as you can, select questions from the bank or from previous papers to answer. It is important to practise questions under the same conditions (exact times) as those you will face in the exam. This exam preparation is one of the most important steps in giving you **confidence to actually do the exam**.

When looking at previous exam papers **look carefully at the rubric** (instructions to the candidate) printed on the front of the paper and under the section headings. Many students have left examinations only to find out later that they did not do a compulsory question. The rubric tells you **how many questions you have to answer in each section, and how long you have to do the paper**. If, for example, you are doing a 3-hour paper and have a 25% extension, you will have 225 minutes. So, for example, if you have to answer four **equal value** questions, your time could be spent as follows:

- 10–15 minutes to select your questions (15 mins).
- For each question:
  o 5 minutes planning (20 mins)
  o 40 minutes writing (160 mins)
  o 7 minutes proofreading (30 mins).

However, if one question is worth 50% of the marks, give it half the time, and split the remainder among the other questions.

All papers require a different distribution of time. If you look at previous papers and practise questions in the time allocated, you will have rehearsed for the examination.

When you have chosen the questions you have decided to practise you should go through the **stages of essay planning**, which have been outlined in Chapter 5. By now you should be able to do this automatically (type of

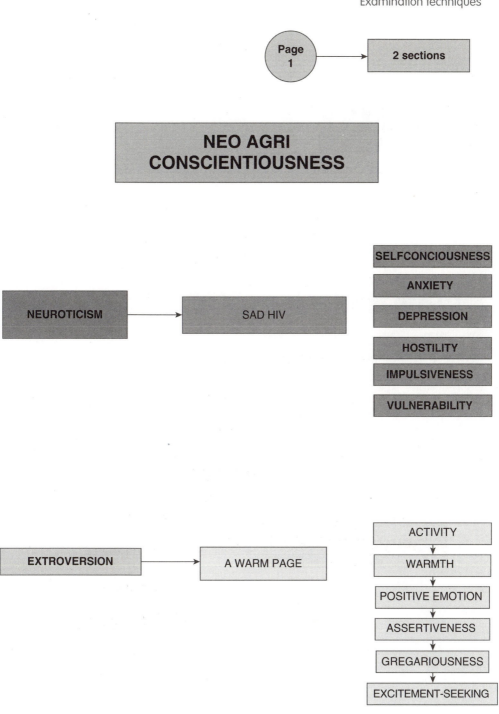

(Continued)

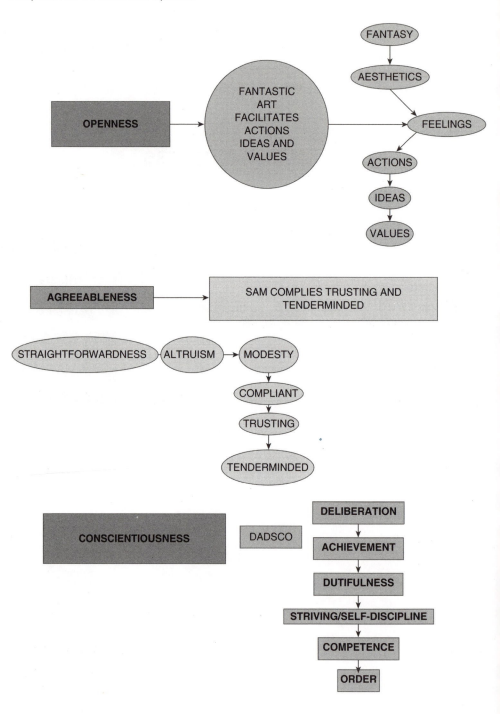

Figure 10.1   Concept map showing creation of personal acronyms as mnemonics to revise psychological terms

question, type of answer, key words, general issues, theme, plan, and essay). If possible, get somebody to read your practice essays and give you feedback. If this is not possible, at least you know that you have managed to complete the required essays in the time available for the examination.

The day before the exam

- Set your alarm to get up at the same time as you want to be up tomorrow.
- Don't look at new material.
- Have a general run through of index cards/Mind Maps™.
- Do some light exercise.
- Drink water and eat healthy food.
- Go to bed at a reasonable time. Don't stay up late studying the night before the examination and skip breakfast or lunch just before the exam to do last-minute revision. This form of cramming is dangerous in two ways:
  - First, you will not remember work you have crammed just before the exam, as it will not have gone into your long-term memory.
  - Secondly, last-minute cramming causes anxiety, and that is not the best mindset in which to take the examination.
- Pack materials for the next day:
  - several pens and pencils, ruler, eraser, etc.
  - a trustworthy watch
  - if you are using a calculator, take spare batteries
  - a bottle of water and banana, sweets, glucose tablets
  - a jumper in case you get cold sitting still for so long.

Sitting the exam

After all this excellent revision and preparation you should have little to worry about.

The final preparations, and those which should ensure that you will be successful, are **to be well rested, well fed, calm and confident**.

Be rested

Fatigue is a danger in examinations, as you will not be working at your greatest potential and recent research has shown that lack of sleep can affect general intelligence.

Recent newspaper articles suggest that people trying to memorise facts and sitting exams should take brief naps as part of their preparation. If you have to sit more than one exam in a day try to have a short 'power nap' between them. Even a few minutes' sleep can help to recharge your batteries.

Be well fed

Failing to eat before exams can cause you to have low blood sugar levels and this may make you feel weak and drowsy. **Eat a nutritious meal at least an hour before you take the exam** so that your body is at its peak, and can support you to perform at your best. If you are taking a long examination, you may wish to take **some dried fruit such as apricots or figs to eat or some still water to drink. Make sure you check that this is allowed under the examination rules at your institution**. If bottles of water are not allowed and the weather is very hot, glasses of water should be made available on request.

Be calm and confident

You should aim to walk into the exam room feeling calm, confident and alert. If you are feeling anxious, try some deep breathing exercises or Brain Gym® (Dennison). If it's a nice day, get off the bus two stops early and walk to college.

During the exam

Regardless of what happens always remain calm and don't become distracted or upset by external problems of any kind. Concentrate on the task.

- Read the rubric (general instructions) carefully.
- Read the whole paper and decide on your choice of questions. Read each question twice. Interpret the questions.
- Consider all key words. Highlight them if you wish.
- Allocate your time according to the number of questions to be answered and the mark value ascribed to each question. Allow time to proofread your answer to each question. Use this time to check spellings, cross out notes or drafts and to check that you have numbered the answer correctly.
- Always answer your best questions first or second in your time allocations to maximise your results.
- Plan your answers and use your time.
- Keep writing.

Strategies to try if your mind goes blank

- Try a relaxation exercise, deep breathing or thinking something pleasant.
- Try writing out the question and ask yourself questions about it. Start simple (Who? What? Why? When? Where? and How?). Now try some more difficult questions.
- Brainstorm a concept map or write key words.
- If you can't remember something when writing, leave a blank in case it comes to you later.
- If all this fails, go to the bathroom and splash water on your face and go back in and try again.
- Don't leave early. Sit there and get through it.

points to remember

In preparing for examinations:

- adopt the right mindset
- make preparations with your institution – Student Services, Assessment Unit
- plan your revision and compile timetables both for the revision period and for the examination period
- revise using the most appropriate methods for your cognitive and learning style
- practise sample examination questions using the methods used in Chapter 5 if essays are required
- check that you know the date, time and room of the exam
- read the whole paper carefully
- allocate your time
- use your time wisely.

CD-ROM Contents

Please go to the CD-ROM accompanying this book to find the following documents:

Exam Timetable	Word Document
Revision Timetable	Word Document
Revision Timetable No. 2	Word Document

Please go to the CD-ROM accompanying this book to find links to the following:

Assignments
How to Build a Memory Palace
How to Improve Your Memory
Memory Improvement Techniques
Method of Loci
Revising, Exams and Assessments
Rhetorica ad Herrenium

11

Collaborative Learning

Paula Baty

developmental objectives

This chapter outlines the main things you need to know about:

- presentations
- group work
- group presentations
- online collaborative work
- role play.

Introduction

Collaborative learning is a situation where people bring their **shared experiences**, **knowledge** and **values** to achieve a **learning goal**. Being actively involved puts into practice what you have learned on your course. Collaborative learning is a great way to **enhance your learning** by learning new and developing existing skills, such as communication skills and working in a team. This chapter first explores **learning actively** through giving oral presentations, and then introduces collaborative learning through group work and role play.

Presentations

Oral presentations are common forms of assessment and it is likely that you will be required to give one (or more) at some stage in your course. Presentations are collaborative in that other students are learning from your work, as you learn from them when they give presentations. Presentations can be particularly stressful for dyslexic students, for fear of stumbling over, or mispronouncing words. They can bring back painful memories of having to read aloud in class. However, many people feel nervous at the thought of public speaking, presentations included (in fact, it's thought to be people's number one fear). It is important to be aware that almost everyone else in your class will feel anxious too, even if they don't look it. Try to look at it as a **positive experience**. Presentations are a good way of **demonstrating your knowledge**. They give you **skills** that are highly prized in the workplace. This section is designed to help you prepare for your presentation. Knowing that you are fully prepared and practised will help you to feel more confident.

Planning your presentation

When planning your presentation, it is important to understand the requirements of the presentation. You can use the marking criteria for your course as a guide. Normally, the marking criteria will contain the following:

- content (how well you demonstrate knowledge of the subject matter).
- structure (ideas set out in a logical and easy-to-follow structure).
- use of visual aids.
- delivery (e.g. voice, body language, eye contact, engaging the audience, pace and timing).
- ability to answer questions.

Look at the allocation of marks. This will give you a good indication of what parts of the presentation are the most important and how to divide your time. (For example the introduction/overview might only be worth a small amount of marks, and while it is important, keep it brief and dedicate more time to more weighty sections.)

Content

The first step, as in writing an essay, is to ensure that you **fully understand the question** and what is required of you. Use a highlighter or pen to highlight/underline key words. **Brainstorm** what you already know about the topic. You might like to create a **Mind Map**™ to help you generate ideas and later structure the presentation. Once you have done a brainstorm, the next step is to do the necessary research (using library books, e-journals, web, etc.) to find further information on your topic. **Formulate questions** to help focus your research. Remember to take a **note** of the sources you use as they will need to be referenced, just as you would in an essay. Keep **referring back** to the topic or question to keep you on track.

Structure

If you have created a Mind Map™ using the popular mind mapping software Inspiration, you can use the Export function to transfer your ideas on the Mind Map™ directly onto a presentation programme, such as Microsoft PowerPoint. It is a quick and easy way of structuring your presentation. If not using Inspiration, you could create a Mind Map™ manually, or draw a flow chart to sequence ideas. Another option is to write your key points onto small cards or Post-It Notes and move them around until you're happy with the order.

Similar to an essay, a presentation contains three main sections: an introduction, body and conclusion.

A general guideline for structuring presentations is:

- Tell them what you're going to tell them (introduction).
- Tell them (body).
- Tell them what you've told them (conclusion).

Introduction This is an overview of the problem/question/topic you're about to tackle and how you will go about doing it.

Body The body will be made up of your key points that will be broken into sections. Try to keep them to a minimum and make sure they contribute directly to the main idea you want to get across to your audience. Use examples and (referenced) quotes to back up your ideas. It's a good idea to use some of the terminology that is specific to your course.

Conclusion Bring the main points together in a clear and concise summary of what you have discussed in your presentation.

Once you have produced an outline of your presentation, ask your tutor to check that you have answered the questions and key concepts and are on the right track.

Using visual aids

Visual aids, such as the presentation software Microsoft PowerPoint, or the open-source version Open Office, are a **valuable** part of your presentation. PowerPoint has become extremely popular as it is very easy to use. A PowerPoint presentation is made up of a number of slides created from layout templates, and the slides can contain text, graphics and videos. PowerPoint is reported to have been invented by a dyslexic person, and it certainly suits the **dyslexic way of thinking**. You can select templates according to the information you want to present. Templates help you to structure your presentation, by organising your ideas into short bullet points under headings. The bullet points act as prompts for your discussion, and if you have additional information you want to remember, but don't want to appear on the slides, there is a notes section where you can add in your notes at the bottom of the screen. You can print off the notes pages separately to act as a prompt while you are presenting. If you want to give handouts to your audience, you can print your slides as a handout. Under Print, you will find the different options, one for Notes Pages and several for the layout of the handouts. Option three is particularly useful as it contains three slides displayed vertically with lines for writing opposite each slide, so that members of your audience can take notes while you are presenting. PowerPoint has many other features – have fun trying them out!

Here's why visual aids are important:

- They add interest to your discussion.
- They enhance and supplement your ideas.
- They take the focus off you, as people will be mainly looking at the slides.
- They help the audience understand what you are talking about.
- They help to demonstrate what you are saying, e.g. graphs.
- They look professional.

In order to use visual aids effectively, consider the following:

- Use headings and bullet points.
- Use diagrams and/or graphs and short video clips to engage interest.
- Avoid cluttering the slides.
- Bullet points should act as prompts for your discussion and should not contain too much information (use the Notes section for additional information).
- How does your presentation look? Think about font size and type, and a background colour that is easily readable.
- Don't overdo the fancy features, such as slide transitions – too many can be distracting and difficult to read.
- Practise with any technology first. Ensure you arrive early on the day of your presentation to make sure the equipment is working properly.

Delivery

Reflect on past presentations you have given – what was successful? What could you improve? Reflect on successful presentations you have been to. What made the presentations interesting, useful, and informative? How did the presenter engage with the audience? Keep these questions in mind when practising the delivery of your presentation.

Practice builds confidence!

As mentioned earlier, if you are fully **prepared** and have **practised** your presentation a number of times, this will help to increase your **confidence** and ease any anxiety. Practise your presentation with a classmate, friend, family member, or learning support tutor. Ask them to give you constructive criticism so that you can make improvements. Learn how to pronounce unfamiliar terminology and difficult vocabulary. Timing is very important as you will lose marks if you are too far under or over the time limit, so time your presentation with a stopwatch or phone. You may then want to either condense your points, or add more information. Sticking to the time limit keeps you from 'waffling' on too much and straying off the topic. It will also help to keep your audience engaged.

Here are some **tips** for presenting on the day:

- Try some relaxation exercises beforehand, such as closing your eyes and taking deep breaths, relaxing the muscles in your neck and shoulders.
- Arrive early to test out your slides and make sure you know what buttons to press, and how to adjust the slides so that they fit the screen.
- Talk to people in the class before your presentation to help ease anxiety.
- Don't stand in front of the screen, and if you need to, read from the laptop or computer, rather than the screen as otherwise your back will be to the audience.
- Interact with your visual aids: they are there to complement your presentation, not replace or contradict them.
- Use the Notes pages or cue cards for supporting information, e.g. additional points/ information, dates, names.
- Try not to fidget or move around too much as this will detract from your discussion.
- Remember to maintain eye contact with your audience.
- Try not to talk too fast – this will make you feel hurried. If you talk more slowly, this can make you feel calmer.

And finally:

- Have a bottle of water handy in case your throat dries out.
- Remember to smile! This will help you to relax.

Answering questions

Knowing that you might have to answer questions in your presentation can be nerve-wracking. However, if you have **practised** beforehand and know your topic well, you have nothing to worry about.

Here are some **suggestions**:

- Anticipate any questions that might be asked – write up a list.
- Try to keep questions to the end so as not to interrupt and throw you off your presentation.
- If you don't know the answer, perhaps ask the audience what they think or ask your lecturer.
- If you don't understand the question, ask them to explain what they mean.
- You don't have to know the answer to everything. You could say: 'interesting question, I don't have the answer right now, but I will look into that'.
- Don't panic!

Presentation checklist

Content

- Do I know my topic well enough?
- Do I feel able to demonstrate my knowledge of the topic?
- Are all my points relevant to the topic?
- Have I backed up my points with examples and explanations?
- Have I included references where necessary?

Structure

- Do I have a clear beginning (intro), middle (body) and end (conclusion) to my presentation?
- Have I given an overview of the presentation in the introduction?
- Do my ideas follow a logical structure? Do they flow from one point to the next?

Delivery

- Can I deliver my presentation within the required time limits?
- Are my ideas paced well?
- Have I practised presenting to a classmate, friend, tutor, or family member?

Use of visual aids

- Have I practised with my slides?
- Are the slides directly relevant to the presentation topic?
- Are my slides easy to read (font size, clear images, etc.)?

Ability to answer questions

- Have I thought about what questions people might ask me?
- Am I prepared for most questions?
- Am I confident in my knowledge of the topic?

Group work

At some stage in your course of study, you will be required to work collaboratively with other students, such as in tutorials, seminars or group presentations or other forms of group work. Through collaborative learning, you can learn **new skills**, such as **working in a team**. Being able to **communicate** and **work effectively as part of a team** is regarded as an **essential** personal skill by employers. Team members bring different knowledge, experiences, values, personalities and qualities to the group, which can be both beneficial and challenging.

Possible challenges

Challenges that can arise in group situations can include: ensuring everyone has the same chance to contribute (some people may dominate, others may hold back); people turning up late or not turning up at all; and conflicting ideas and personalities.

Solutions

Establishing **ground rules** from the very first meeting can help your group to avoid possible conflict. For example:

Work out roles	Take into consideration individual strengths and weaknesses (e.g. if you are worried about being the note-taker, take on a role you feel more comfortable with).
Divide responsibilities	Make sure that responsibilities and tasks are divided fairly.
Clarify assessment tasks	Get to know your task. Break it down into sub-tasks. Identify what parts can be done independently and what parts are interdependent. You should have an agreed approach in terms of steps to be taken and a timeline/ to do list to show what tasks need to be done and when.
Organisation	Meeting dates should be set in advance, with clear goals, and how it will work.
Forms of communication	Meetings, email, phone, tutorials, WebCT/ Blackboard. Remember, communication is key.

Possible challenges for the dyslexic student

Group work can be particularly stressful for dyslexic students, as they might be worried about their spelling and grammar, note-taking, speaking and pronunciation.

Solutions

Spelling and grammar	If you are worried about your spelling and grammar, you could try to make light of it by saying something like, 'spelling isn't really my strong point' and ask someone in your group to check it for you.
Listening and note-taking	Listen actively – take notes when listening to others (by hand using bullet points or a Mind Map™, or using a laptop), or record the meetings.
Speaking and pronunciation	Practise with a friend, family member or learning support tutor. Learn the pronunciation of unfamiliar and difficult terminology. You could jot down some bullet points in advance and plan what you want to say. Or talk through a Mind Map™ to help you express your ideas (this has worked well for students in the past, and they have found that the group loves the Mind Map™ idea and have even included them in their presentations!).
Listening and interpersonal skills	Play a big part. Think about your body language, give others time to talk, and encourage them while they're speaking.
Nerves	Try to enjoy the process. Your team is there to support and encourage each other.

Group presentations

In contrast to individual presentations where you are learning from each other in the course but are solely responsible for, and in control of, the entire presentation, group presentations are a collaborative effort. You will each be required to research and present a section of the presentation. When introducing the presentation, give an **overview** and tell the audience who will be talking about each section. Ensure your **ideas flow** coherently to make smooth transitions from one speaker to the next.

Assessment

In addition to the marking criteria (content, structure, delivery, use of visual aids, and the ability to answer questions) for individual presentations given in the previous section, it is likely that the **marking criteria** for group presentations will also include:

- group dynamics
- group collaboration
- working effectively as a team
- evidence of co-operation
- communication.

Bear this in mind when planning your presentation. As with any form of group work, as mentioned above, it is important to set out **ground rules** from the beginning in order to plan and deliver a successful presentation.

Online collaborative learning

Online learning (in a web-based environment) is now widely used in colleges and universities. Find out if it will be used on your course and to what extent. Some courses are run solely through online learning. This type of learning is very **flexible** as it allows you to learn at your own pace, in your own time. The learning management system, commonly known as Blackboard or WebCT, not only enables you to access information and resources, it allows you to **engage** and **interact** with other students and lecturers/tutors in your courses. There are several ways through which you can participate in online learning through Blackboard/WebCT:

Discussion boards, chats and virtual classrooms This is where you can discuss ideas with others.

Group pages Your course leader might form groups in order to do activities that you will be required to participate in.

Blogs	These are websites that focus on a particular topic that you are able to comment on.
Wikis	These are a type of collaborative web space which can be edited by groups.
Journals	Reflective journals are used for your own personal reflection and can only be accessed by you and your lecturer/tutor.
Podcast	Your tutor/lecturer might post podcasts which are video or audio segments on a particular topic. You are able to comment on the podcasts.
Skype	This is also sometimes used for online group learning, as you can set up group video 'conferences'. Skype is accessed through the internet and Skype to Skype communication is free.

If this all sounds daunting, don't be put off, as online collaborative learning can be very **rewarding**. Make sure you ask someone to show you how to use the technology. Your college or university's website may have a **demonstration**, or ask library or other staff or your classmates.

Role play

Role play is an effective method of learning, particularly for students on **practical courses and placements**, such as nurses, social workers, dieticians and teachers. Through role play you can put your knowledge into practice and develop practical skills, which will enable you to gain confidence. The skills and strategies learnt can then be **transferred to the professional context**, not only while you are studying, but in future employment. Role play can also be useful for students not on practical courses. For example, it can be **a valuable way of preparing for presentations and interviews**. Before you begin, think about **what your goals are and what you are aiming to achieve**. Think about the particular skills that you would like to develop. With this in mind, see how you can incorporate role play into your learning.

Using role play on practice placements

While **practice placements** are a great opportunity for you to put the theory learnt on your course into practice, they can pose potential **challenges** for students with dyslexia, dyspraxia or other specific learning difficulties. Figure 11.1 shows some areas that you might like to **develop**, and **solutions** that involve **collaborating** with a partner.

Goals	Solutions
Developing interpersonal skills	Role play different scenarios with a partner, considering body language, tone and volume of voice, and eye contact. Prepare some points you would like to get across first – jot down using bullet points.
Pronouncing new terminology	Create a checklist of unfamiliar vocabulary/new terminology and practise how to say those words with a partner. You could also record them saying the words so you can practise on your own later.
Understanding new terminology	Ask a partner or tutor for clarification if you are unsure of any new terminology. Create a glossary of new terminology and revise it regularly (using multi-sensory techniques; see Chapter 2) to commit it to your long-term memory.
Understanding/following instructions	Repeat the instructions back to your supervisor to check that you have understood them. Ask for instructions to be repeated one at a time and write them down if you can (into a notebook, diary or organiser), or use a recording device.
Remembering what questions to ask	Draw up a checklist of standard questions you might need to ask a patient/client. Become familiar with these questions by practising with a partner.

Figure 11.1   Using role play on practice placements

Using role play: a case study

This section demonstrates the use of role play in a certain context – in this instance, on a placement as a dietician. By its very nature role play lends itself to being explained though a specific example. Discussion on how role play can be used in other contexts, such as teaching, will be given towards the end of the chapter. You may well be able to **apply the ideas to your course of study**.

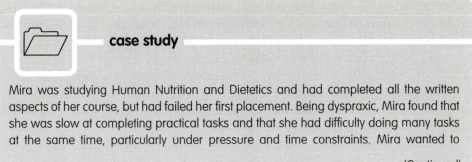

case study

Mira was studying Human Nutrition and Dietetics and had completed all the written aspects of her course, but had failed her first placement. Being dyspraxic, Mira found that she was slow at completing practical tasks and that she had difficulty doing many tasks at the same time, particularly under pressure and time constraints. Mira wanted to

(Continued)

(Continued)

improve her skills and be equipped with strategies to help overcome her difficulties, and ultimately pass her course.

As a dietician, Mira was required to know a lot of detailed information, such as the breakdown of foods, serving sizes, and biochemistry. It was essential that she could access this information from memory when seeing clients.

Mira's main difficulties were with remembering what to ask a client during a consultation, while at the same time calculating calories according to food portions, and maintaining eye contact. She would often 'lose track' of what question she was going to ask next. She was also concerned about her slowness at these tasks, and the need to appear confident and professional. After the consultation, Mira would be required to enter the client information on a record card, which also gave her cause for concern as she had difficulty with correctly ordering the information. Above all, since having failed her placement, she lacked self-confidence.

After discussing what her main areas of need were, Mira and her tutor decided that a useful way to develop the skills necessary for her intended profession and to practise 'being a dietician' would be through role play. They simulated consultations with 'clients' (tutor) with different medical conditions so that Mira could have practice in a variety of situations. This was supplemented with pre- and follow-up activities, such as filling out record cards after the 'consultation'.

Applying what she had learnt on her course to real-life situations helped Mira to develop her skills and demonstrate her knowledge, which in turn helped greatly to rebuild her confidence and pass the placement.

Here are some suggestions that Mira found worked for her.

Preparation

Read through the client's previous record notes and jot down key points onto a pad in the correct order (for example, date order with the most recent information first). Ask yourself questions: What is this person's medical history? What information do I already know? What do I need to find out? What questions am I going to ask, and in what order?

If this is the client's first consultation and there are no previous record notes, you might like to **draw up a checklist** on a piece of card so that you can enter essential information onto it. Take this into the consultation to help you remember what information you need to find out. Figure 11.2 provides an example of a general checklist.

You might like **to make up a series of cards** for different medical conditions where more specific information is needed. The **cards could be colour coded** and you could use pictures to illustrate them. You could try using other colour coded cards to help you remember what questions you may need to

Age: _____
Weight: _____
Height: _____
BMI (Body Mass Index): _____
Additional information:
_____
_____
_____
_____
_____

Figure 11.2   Patient checklist

ask. For example, if you need to find out a client's daily food intake you could write down what you need to ask (in order) onto a card, such as in Figure 11.3. **Visual association can help to aid recall, so it may be helpful to draw diagrams linked to your questions**. After a while, you might find that you don't need to use the cards all the time, as you are able to remember each question by visualising the associated picture.

Using a **personal organiser** can be helpful, not only for organising your time and workload, but also for storing important information. Among other things, Mira included in her personal organiser a list of food portion sizes, which she needed in order to calculate calories and suggest meal plans for clients.

1. First meal of the day: _____
    _____
2. Anything before lunch? _____
    _____
3. Lunch: _____
    _____
4. Anything before dinner? _____
    _____
5. Dinner: _____
    _____
6. Anything else? _____

Figure 11.3   Daily food intake

Using a case study as a basis for your role play

As you are trying to practise being in a real-life situation, why not try **using real-life case studies**? The internet is a useful resource for this, and you can find Question and Answer (Q&A) pages where people have written in to get advice from doctors and health professionals, or you may have case studies in your course books. **Case studies provide good, real examples**, which you can use as a basis for your role play.

Alternatively, **try using an internet search engine** to find an article on a particular subject, for example Crohn's disease. This can be good reading practice for you too. Try skim reading the article, highlighting key words and/or jotting down key words or sentences onto a piece of paper. (For more reading strategies, see Chapter 4.) Then, think about what information you would need to find out from a client with Crohn's disease. You may like to use a checklist as suggested above to help you.

See what you can find – be creative!

Rehearsing your role play

The next step is to put **all your preparation into practice** in a role play. You could try this with your learning support tutor, friend, family member or classmate.

Your **role play partner can assume the role of the patient or client**, with whatever illness or medical condition you choose. Try a variety to test your knowledge – an overweight, middle-aged man with heart problems, a pregnant woman, a person with diabetes, or an older person with malnutrition.

Try to relax and don't worry about making mistakes – learning is all about 'trial and error'! Assume your role, and remember to be professional as you are trying to mirror a possible real-life situation. Use your checklists to help you remember what you need to ask. As you go along, make notes onto your checklist card or a notepad. If you need to calculate calories, do this at the end so that you do not lose track of the questions you are asking. Next, discuss with your client what you have found out from their answers. Try giving them advice and recommendations. For example, if your client is an overweight, middle-aged male, try suggesting ways that he can lower his calorie intake. This would be a useful way to demonstrate your expertise.

Follow-up activities

A **useful follow-up exercise** could be to suggest a meal plan for the client. You could write down a meal plan for a week of a healthier diet and give this to them, explaining the reasons for your recommendations. Practise doing calorie calculations for this also.

Then fill out the client's record card with your notes from the consultation. If this is the client's first record card, enter their general details (age, weight, height, BMI) in first at the top of the card. Use your checklists to help you.

Other uses of role play

As mentioned, role play is **particularly useful for students on practical courses and placements**, such as dieticians, doctors, nurses, social workers, teachers, etc. If you are training to be a teacher, for example, think of how you could incorporate role play into the classroom. In a history lesson, students could have great fun **acting out scenes in history,** or pretending to be a prime minister giving an historical speech. In English lessons, students can take on the **roles of characters in novels and plays** and be asked questions by the class about their reasons for certain actions.

In order to monitor how you come across to your pupils in your role as a teacher, it can be useful to **tape record yourself when you are in the classroom**. Take note of the **tone and pitch of your voice** – what effect does it have on the students in the class? Is your speech calm, clear and even? What is your rate of speech – are you talking too quickly? Are you easy to understand? If you **videotape yourself giving a lesson**, notice your pupils' reactions to what you are saying. Are they responding positively? What things could you do to improve?

Role play is an **integral part of learning a new language**. Try **acting out different scenarios** such as ordering food from a restaurant, buying train tickets, and introducing yourself at a party. Think about your intonation and pronunciation as well.

If you are not on a practice-based course, think of how role play can be useful for you. If you need to give a presentation, rehearse it in front of someone, such as a family member. If you are going for a **job interview, try role playing** the interview with someone. Ask them to **give you feedback** on what went well, and what you need to develop. Why not try **explaining a concept** to a friend, family member or classmate? Talk it through with them. Not only will this help you to demonstrate your knowledge, but they might learn something new also!

 **points to remember**

- Being fully prepared and practised for your presentation will help you to feel more confident.
- Visual aids, such as PowerPoint, help you to structure your presentation, add interest and enhance your ideas.

- Through group work, you can develop valuable skills such as working in a team.
- Online learning provides a flexible way of engaging and interacting with others on your course.
- Put your knowledge into practice by incorporating role play into your learning.

CD-ROM Contents

Please go to the CD-ROM accompanying this book to find links to the following:

Developing Listening and Interpersonal Skills
Learn Higher Group Work – Resources for Students
Making Group-work Work
Oral Communication, Participating in Seminars, Preparing and Giving Presentations
Role Play in Presentations
Working in Groups – Deakin University

Glossary

Abbreviation   Shortening something by omitting parts of it.

Abstract   A summary of the main points of an argument or theory.

Acronyms   A word formed from the initial letters of a multi-word name.

AlphaSmart   A portable computer keyboard which you can use and then download to a PC.

Amanuensis   Someone skilled in the transcription of speech (especially dictation).

Analysis   The process of breaking a complex topic or substance into smaller parts to gain a better understanding of it.

Analytic   Using or skilled in using analysis (i.e. separating a whole – intellectual or substantial – into its elemental parts or basic principles).

Argumentative   Given to or characterised by argument; 'an argumentative discourse'.

Articulating   Uttering distinct syllables or words.

Auditory   Of or relating to the process of hearing; 'auditory processing'.

Bibliography   Alphabetical reference list at end of an essay or course work.

Blog   A website that focuses on a particular topic that you are able to comment on.

Bottom up   Looking at something analytically rather than holistically.

Brainstorming   Thinking intensely about a topic or theme and recording the ideas.

Chunking   Grouping together in compact sections.

Citation   A short note acknowledging a source of information or quoting a passage.

Clause   An expression including a subject and verb but not constituting a complete sentence.

Cognitive style   Thinking style.

Collaborative learning   A situation where people bring their shared experiences, knowledge and values to achieve a learning goal.

Concept mapping   A map of abstract or general ideas inferred or derived from specific instances.

Concrete materials   Capable of being perceived by the senses; not abstract or imaginary.

Condensing   Reducing or compacting.

Deadline   The point in time at which something must be completed.

Discussion boards, chats and virtual classrooms   Online forums where you can discuss your ideas with others.

Dissertation or **thesis**   A document submitted in support of candidature for an academic degree or professional qualification presenting the author's research and findings.

Endnote   Footnote at the end of a chapter or section.

Errors   Inadvertent incorrectness.

Evaluative   Appraising; exercising or involving careful evaluations.

Explanatory   Serving or intended to explain or make clear.

Expository   Serving to expound or set forth.

Footnote   A note placed below the text on a printed page.

Genre   A style of expressing yourself in writing.

Grasshopper   One who looks at issues holistically.

Group pages   Online groups in which to participate in activities.

Holistic   Emphasising the organic or functional relation between parts and the whole.

HTML   Hyper Text Mark-up Language.

Illustrations   A visual representation (a picture or diagram) that is used to make some subject more pleasing or easier to understand.

Imagery   The ability to form mental images of things or events; usually related to the senses.

Inchworm   A thinking process which moves analytically from the bottom up.

Index cards   Coloured cards which can be used to store information and sorted in different ways.

Information processing   Thinking about information and organising it.

Integers   Numbers.

Interactive   Capable of acting on or influencing each other.

Interpretative   To make sense of or assign a meaning to.

Journal (online)   Used for your own personal reflection and can only be accessed by you and your lecturer/tutor.

Kinaesthetic   Of or relating to the process of movement; 'kinaesthetic processing'. A 'hands-on' approach to things.

Learning management system   A type of online learning system, such as *Blackboard* or *WebCT*.

Learning style   The way one learns.

Linear notes   Notes which are kept in sequential lines rather than patterns.

Listening comprehension   An ability to understand the meaning or importance of something (or the knowledge acquired as a result) through listening.

Literature review   A review of the books available on a specific topic.

Memory pegs   A set or group of thoughts which trigger other thoughts.

Metacognitive   Knowing how you think.

Methodology   The system of methods followed in a particular discipline.

Mindfulness   Involves paying attention to thoughts and feelings in a way that can increase our awareness of how to manage difficult experiences, and make wise choices.

Mind Mapping™   Term coined by Tony Buzan to indicate the grouping of concepts relating to a topic.

Mnemonics   A method or system for improving the memory.

Motivation   A positive and proactive desire to do something.

Morphology   The structure of words.

Multi-sensory   Applying learning strategies that draw upon more than one of the senses (visual, auditory and kinaesthetic) to aid learning.

Object   The noun or pronoun after a verb or preposition.

Overview   A holistic view of the whole work.

Passive   The voice used to indicate that the subject of the verb is the recipient (not the source) of the action denoted by the verb.

PDA   Personal digital assistant.

PDF   Portable Document Format – Adobe Acrobat.

PEST/STEP   Political, Economic, Social and Technological aspects of a subject.

Plagiarism   Use of another person's ideas or findings as your own by simply copying them or reproducing them without due acknowledgement.

PowerPoint projection   The projection of a presentation from a computer onto a screen made in PowerPoint.

Phonetics   Relating to the scientific study of speech sounds.

Phonology   The study of the sound system of a given language and the analysis and classification of its phonemes.

Podcast   Video or audio segments on a particular topic.

Prioritise   Assign a priority to.

Prioritised reading list   Reading lists in which the most important books are clearly indicated.

Punctuation   The use of certain marks to clarify meaning of written material by grouping words grammatically into sentences and clauses and phrases.

Q Notes   A way of taking notes suggested by Jim Bourke, in which a question is asked and an answer provided.

Questionnaire   A form containing a set of questions; submitted to people in order to gain statistical information.

Reading comprehension   An ability to understand the meaning or importance of something (or the knowledge acquired as a result) through reading.

Referencing   Acknowledgement of a source of information.

Role play   The rehearsal of a specific scenario.

Roots   Square root – number which when multiplied by itself equals a given number. Cube root – a number which when multiplied three times equals a given number.

Rubric   A heading that is printed in red or in a special type. The overall instructions on exam papers.

Sans serif   A font style which is plain and without loops.

Scheduled   Planned or scheduled for some certain time or times; 'the scheduled lectures'.

Self-esteem   A person's perception of their self-worth and abilities.

Semester   One of two divisions of an academic year. Half a year; a period of six months.

Sigma   The sum of a set of numbers.

Simultaneously   At the same time.

Skype   An application that is used for video conferencing and instant messaging.

Squared   A number multiplied by itself.

Standard deviation   Statistical measure of spread or variability.

Statistics   A branch of applied mathematics concerned with the collection and interpretation of quantitative data and the use of probability theory to estimate population parameters.

Strategies   Systematic plans of action.

Subject   The noun or pronoun before the verb.

Sub-vocalising   To verbalise silently.

SWOT   Strengths, Weaknesses, Opportunities and Threats.

Synthesis   Combining ideas into a complex whole.

Techniques   A practical method applied to some particular task.

Template   A model or standard for making comparisons.

Top down   Looking at things holistically, from the top.

Trigger (memory)   Any thought that sets in motion a range of other thoughts.

Unpacking the question   Methods of making the question easier to understand. Analysing it in sections.

URL   Universal Resource Locator (letters you write in the bar after www. to locate a website).

Verbalising   To think or express in words.

Visual   Relating to or using sight; 'visual powers'; 'visual navigation'. Able to be seen; 'a visual presentation'; 'a visual image'.

Visualising   Thinking in visual images.

Viva Voce   An oral presentation followed by oral questions and answers.

Viva (Voice)   An examination where questions are asked and answered orally rather than a written paper.

Well-being   Maintaining good physical and mental health for a happy and healthy life.

Wiki   A type of collaborative web space which can be edited by groups.

References and Further Reading

If you have found this book helpful, you might also find other similar books useful. As a start you could try the following books, many of which were referred to in this volume. In addition, there is a list of websites that might also be of interest.

Berners-Lee, T. (1999) *Weaving the Web: The Original Design and Ultimate Destiny of the World Wide Web By Its Inventor*. San Francisco: HarperOne.

Brown, R.B. and Saunders, M. (2008) *Dealing with Statistics: What You Need to Know*. Open University Press, Maidenhead: Open University Press.

Brunel University (2007) *Oral Communication*. Available at: www.brunel.ac.uk/learnhigher/giving-oral-presentations/considering-your-audience.shtml

Burke, J. (2002) *Tools for Thought*. Portsmouth, NH: Heinemann.

Burns, T. and Sinfield, S. (2002) *Essential Study Skills*. London: SAGE Publications.

Buzan, T. (1988) *Make the Most of Your Mind* (rev. edition). London: Pan Books.

Buzan, T. (1995) *Use Your Head* (4th edition). London: BBC.

Buzan, T. (2004) *The Speed Reading Book*. London: BBC.

Buzan, T. and Buzan, B. (2006) *The Mind Map Book* (rev. edition). London: BBC Active.

Chambers, P. and Tovey, M. (2004) *Radiant Thinking Skills*. Bucknell: Learning Technologies Ltd.

Chinn, S.J. and Ashcroft, J.R. (1998) *Mathematics for Dyslexics: A Teaching Handbook* (2nd edition). London: Whurr.

Cottrell, S. (2003) *The Study Skills Handbook* (2nd edition). Basingstoke: Palgrave Macmillan.

Cottrell, S. (2005) *Critical Thinking Skills*. Basingstoke: Palgrave Macmillan.

Creme, P. (2000) 'The "personal" in university writing: uses of reflective learning journals', in M.R. Lea and B. Stierer (eds) *Student Writing in Higher Education: New Contexts*. Buckingham: The Society for Research in Higher Education/Open University Press.

Deakin University (2011) *Working in Groups*. Available at: www.deakin.edu.au/current-students-study-support/study-skills/handouts/groups.php/

Dennison, P. (1994) *Switching On: The Whole Brain Answer to Dyslexia*. Ventura, CA: Edu-Kinesthetics Inc.

Dennison, P. and Dennison, G. (1992) *Brain Gym: Simple Activities for Whole Brain Learning*. Ventura, CA: Edu-Kinesthetics Inc.

Dennison, P. and Dennison, G. (1994) *Brain Gym: Teacher's Edition Revised*. Ventura, CA: Edu-Kinesthetics Inc.

Dennison, P. and Dennison, G. (1995) *Educational Kinesiology In-Depth: The Seven Dimensions of Intelligence*. Ventura, CA: Edu-Kinesthetics Inc.

Du Pré, L., Gilroy, D. and Miles, T. (2007a) *Dyslexia at College* (3rd edition). London: Routledge.

Du Pré, L., Gilroy, D. and Miles, T. (2007b) 'Organising yourself and your time', in *Dyslexia at College* (3rd edition). London: Routledge.

Foer, J. (2011) *Moonwalking with Einstein: The Art and Science of Remembering Everything*. Longon: Penguin.

Gilroy, D.E. and Miles, T.R (1996) *Dyslexia at College* (2nd edition). London Routledge.

Goodwin, V. and Thomson, B. (2004) *Making Dyslexia Work for You*. London: David Fulton Publishers.

Grant, D. (2010) *That's the Way I Think: Dyslexia and Dyspraxia Explained* (2nd edition). London: Routledge.

Greetham, B. (2001) *How to Write Better Essays*. Basingtoke: Palgrave.

Jarvie, G. (2000) *Bloomsbury Grammar Guide: Grammar Made Easy*. London: Bloomsbury.

Kabat-Zinn, J. (2004) *Wherever You Go, There You Are: Mindfulness Meditation for Everyday Life*. London: Piatkus.

McLoughlin, D., Leather, C. and Stringer, P. (2003) *The Adult Dyslexic*. London: Whurr.

Mortimore, T. (2003) *Dyslexia and Learning Style*. London: Whurr.

Ott, P. (1997) *How to Detect and Manage Dyslexia*. London: Heinemann.

Pauk, W. (2001) *How to Study in College* (7th edition). Boston, MA: Houghton Mifflin Company.

Pleuger, G. (ed.) (2000) *The Good History Student's Handbook*. Bedford: Sempringham.

Pollak, D. (ed.) (2009) *Neurodiversity in Higher Education*. Chichester: John Wiley.

Pollak, D. and McCrea, K. (eds) (2009) 'Mental well-being', in D. Pollak (ed.) *Neurodiversity in Higher Education*. Chichester: John Wiley.

Puddicombe, A. (2011) *Get Some Headspace (10 Minutes Can Make All the Difference)*. London: Hodder & Stoughton.

Riding, R.J. and Rayner, S. (1998) *Cognitive Styles and Learning Strategies*. London: David Fulton Publishers.

Slattery, M. and Pleuger, G. (2000) 'Essay planning: early steps', in G. Pleuger (ed.) *The Good History Student's Handbook*. Bedford: Sempringham.

Smythe, I. (2009) *Dyslexia in the Digital Age: Making IT Work*. London: Continuum.

Symonds, H. (2008) 'Introducing oral assessment within creative practice: "I can write but it's like walking against the wind".' *Journal of Writing in Creative Practice*, 1(3).

Truss, L. (2003) *Eats, Shoots and Leaves*. London: Profile Books.

University of Aukland (no date) *Presentation Concerns*. Available at: www.cad.auckland.ac.nz/index.php?p=pc

University of Essex (2000) *Assessment Criteria for Oral Communication*. Avilable at: www.essex.ac.uk/assessment/oral%20assessment_criteria.htm

University of Hull (2007) *Handy Study Tips*. Available at: www2.hull.ac.uk/student/studyadvice/studyskillsresources/handystudytips.aspx

Walliman, N. (2005) *Your Undergraduate Dissertation*. London: SAGE Publications.

West, T.G. (1991) *In the Mind's Eye: Visual Thinkers, Gifted People with Learning Difficulties, Computer Images and the Ironies of Creativity*. New York: Prometheus Books.

West, T.G. (2004) *Thinking Like Einstein: Returning to our Visual Roots with the Emerging Revolution in Computer Information Visualization*. New York: Prometheus Books.

Useful websites

Concept Stew Ltd *Educational Software Design and Development* [online]. Available from: www.conceptstew.co.uk/PAGES/home.html

Coping with exam stress: www.isma.org.uk/exams.htm

Deakin University's links to advice on working in groups, including online group work: http://www.deakin.edu.au/current-students/study-support/study-skills/handouts/groups.php/

Examination arrangements: www.qub.ac.uk/directorates/sgc/disability/services/Examinationsupport/

Examination techniques: www.mantex.co.uk/software/skill-01.htm

Help Guide (2011) Helpguide.org: Expert, free articles help empower you with knowledge, support & hope. *Help Guide*. Available at: http://helpguide.org/

LearnHigher has tips and activities on group work: http://learnhigher.ac.uk/Students/Group-work.html

Learning Technologies Ltd: www.learning-tech.co.uk

MathsisFun: www.mathsisfun.com

Mind Tools (2011). Available at: http://www.mindtools.com/

Purdue University's Online Writing Lab. Available at: http://owl.english.purdue.edu/

Psychology Today (2011) Psych Basics: Core concepts in the field of psychology. *Psychology Today*. Available at: http://www.psychologytoday.com/basics

Puddicombe, A. (2011) Headspace: Meditate and be mindful. Learn Meditation and Mindfulness. How to meditate with Headspace. *Get Some Headspace*. Available at: http://www.getsomeheadspace.com/

Q *Notes* by Jim Burke (2000): www.englishcompanion.com

Study skills, Leicester University: Interactive Study Guide: http://www2.le.ac.uk/offices/ssds/accessability/study-skills

Style guide: www.timesonline.co.uk/tol/tools_and_services/specials/style_guide/article986718.ece

Style guide: www.guardian.co.uk/styleguide/

Style guide: www.mathsisfun.com

TechDis aims to enhance provision for disabled students and staff in higher, further and specialist education and adult and community learning, through the use of technology: www.jisctechdis.ac.uk

Tips and activities on developing listening and interpersonal skills (LearnHigher): http://learnhigher.ac.uk/Students/Listening-and-interpersonal-skills.html

Tips on using role-play in presentations from Brunel University: http://www.brunel.ac.uk/learnhigher/giving-oral-presentations/Roleplay.pdf

Tips on oral communication, including participating in seminars and preparing and giving presentations. Brunel University (2007) Oral Communication. Available at: http://www.brunel.ac.uk/learnhigher/giving-oral-presentations/considering-your-audience.shtml.

University of Leeds have developed a web-based video resource entitled 'Making Group-work Work': http://skills.library.leeds.ac.uk/topic_group_work.php

University of Reading (2011) Getting organised – University of Reading. Available at: http://www.reading.ac.uk/internal/studyadvice/StudyResources/Time/sta-organised.aspx

University of Southampton Study Skills Site (2003) www.soton.ac.uk/ studentsupport/ldc/academicskills/study.html

Index

IMPROVING WORKING MEMORY

Supporting Students' Learning

Tracy Packiam Alloway *University of North Florida*

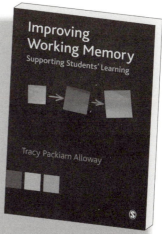

Your working memory is the information your brain stores for a short period of time, it is your brain's post-it note if you like, and how much information you can remember has a huge influence on how well you do at school, and beyond.

By developing and improving a child's working memory, you will see improvements in their achievements at school, and in their concentration. Better working memory can be particularly useful to children with conditions where poor working memory is thought to be an underlying factor. Such conditions include:

- dyslexia
- dyscalculia
- speech and language difficulties
- developmental coordination disorders (motor dyspraxia)
- ADHD (attention deficit hyperactivity disorder)
- autistic spectrum disorders

This book explains how to spot problems early, and how to work with children to improve their working memory, therefore increasing their chances of success in the classroom. It is packed full of practical strategies to use with students, but it also explains the theory behind these activities.

Underpinned by rigorous research and written in a highly accessible style, this book will appeal to practitioners, parents and students as an essential guide to helping their students fulfil their maximum potential.

CONTENTS

Our Brain's Post-It-Note \ Diagnosing Working Memory \ Reading Disorder \ Mathematical Disorder \ Dyspraxia \ ADHD \ Autistic Spectrum Disorder \ Student Strategies and Training

2010 • 136 pages
Cloth (978-1-84920-747-8) • £69.00
Paper (978-1-84920-748-5) • £22.99
Electronic (978-1-4462-4796-9) • £22.99

ALSO FROM SAGE!

TEACHING LITERACY TO LEARNERS WITH DYSLEXIA

A Multi-sensory Approach

Kathleen Kelly *Manchester Metropolitan University* and **Sylvia Phillips** *Glyndwr University*

Providing a structured programme for teaching literacy to children and young people with dyslexia and specific literacy difficulties, this book makes explicit links between theory, research and practice. It offers a structured, cumulative, multi-sensory teaching programme for learners with dyslexia, and draws attention to some of the wider aspects of the learning styles and differences of learners with dyslexia such as memory, information processing and automaticity.

The book discusses:

- the rationale for a structured multi-sensory approach
- the development of phonological, reading, writing and spelling skills
- working with learners who have English as an additional language (EAL)
- lesson structure and lesson-planning
- alphabet and dictionary skills
- memory work and study skills
- teaching the programme to groups
- ideas for working with young children.

Designed to help support any learner, from ages five to 18, with dyslexia or specific learning difficulties, the authors encourage the use of the programme as part of everyday teaching to not only develop literacy but to put dyslexic learners in control of their own learning.

September 2011 • 424 pages
Cloth (978-0-85702-534-0) • £85.00
Paper (978-0-85702-535-7) • £29.99
Electronic (978-1-4462-5393-9) • £29.99

ALSO FROM SAGE!

THE DYSLEXIA-FRIENDLY PRIMARY SCHOOL

A Practical Guide for Teachers

Barbara Pavey *Freelance Consultant*

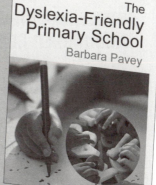

Is your school dyslexia-friendly?

Beginning with a look at understanding dyslexia, this book shows you how to involve the whole school in order to achieve a dyslexia-friendly environment.

You will be able to:

- use an audit tool to discover how dyslexia-friendly your school is
- look at examples of successful dyslexia-friendly initiatives
- find information on funding and resources

This book offers a step-by-step guide to creating a dyslexia-friendly classroom and whole-school environment.

Headteachers, deputy headteachers, class teachers, SENCOs, student teachers and literacy co-ordinators wanting to make their school more dyslexia-friendly will find this practical book extremely useful.

Barbara Pavey worked as a teacher and SEN specialist for many years and is now Lecturer in Learning Disabilities at The University of Manchester.

CONTENTS

Understanding Dyslexia \ The Dyslexia-Friendly Initiative \ Funding and Resources \ Policies, Principles, Practices and Processes \ The Family View \ Dyslexia-Friendliness \ How Dyslexia-Friendly Is My Primary School? \ The Way Forward

READERSHIP

Headteachers, deputy headteachers, class teachers, SENCOs, student teachers and literacy co-ordinators

2007 • 120 pages
Cloth (978-1-4129-1029-3) • £71.00
Paper (978-1-4129-1030-9) • £21.99
Electronic (978-1-84860-744-6) • £21.99

NEW FROM SAGE!

DYSLEXIA-FRIENDLY FURTHER AND HIGHER EDUCATION

Barbara Pavey *Freelance Consultant*, **Margaret Meehan** *University of Swansea* and **Alan Waugh** *Programme Area Manager for Additional Support at City College, Coventry*

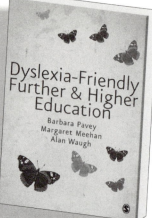

Written by authors with extensive experience of working with students with dyslexia, this book provides clear guidance and practical strategies for dyslexia-friendly practice for those working with young people aged 14 to 19 and adults in education or work-based training.

Looking at how dyslexia impacts on learning, the authors suggest ways to improve the learning environment and explain how to help students develop the basic skills that will help them to make the transition from study to employment. Building on the latest research and understanding of dyslexia, they also consider overlapping characteristics, emotional and social issues and funding.

The book includes:

- visual chapter summaries
- case studies drawn from practice
- ideas for dyslexia-friendly written work, and lab and bench work
- international perspectives
- a selection of resources
- model lesson plans and useful checklists

This is essential reading not only for those studying dyslexia-focused programmes at Master's level, but also for mainstream practitioners wishing to improve their dyslexia knowledge and practice, and an ideal resource for professionals working in a school, college, university or adult setting, or delivering training and consultancy in this field.

2009 • 136 pages
Cloth (978-1-84787-585-3) • £75.00
Paper (978-1-84787-586-0) • £24.99
Electronic (978-1-4462-0595-2) • £24.99

ALSO FROM SAGE!